SO-AFE-742

CHEN STYLE
TAIJIQUAN

Compiled by ZHAOHUA PUBLISHING HOUSE

HAI FENG PUBLISHING CO. Hong Kong
&
ZHAOHUA PUBLISHING HOUSE Beijing, China

Cover: Li Shiji

© Hai Feng Publishing Co., 1984

ISBN 962-238-016-6

Published by
HAI FENG PUBLISHING CO.
Rm. 701, Chung Shang Bldg. 7/F.
9-10, Queen Victoria St.
Hong Kong

        and

ZHAOHUA PUBLISHING HOUSE
Chegongzhuang Xilu 21
Beijing, China

Printed by
C & C JOINT PRINTING CO. (H.K.) LTD.
75, Pau Chung St.
Kowloon, Hong Kong

First Edition 1984

All rights reserved

7·297-24   00400   7-E-1681p

CONTENTS

The Origin, Evolution and Development of Shadow Boxing

By Gu Liuxin, Deputy Director and researcher
of the Shanghai Institute of Physical Culture

1.   The Origin of Shadow Boxing

Shadow boxing (*taijiquan*) is one of the famous branches of Chinese martial arts. More than 300 years have passed since its spread at the beginning of the Qing Dynasty. Its immense popularity in Beijing around the time the 1911 Revolution, however, gave rise to the saying that the pugilist art was passed down to the secular world by celestial beings; and, as a result, the date of the origin of shadow boxing was shifted several centuries earlier, from the 17th century to the 15th, 12th and even 8th century. "An Illustrated Book of Shadow Boxing" (shadow boxing of the Yang school) published in Beijing in 1921, for example, attributes the origin of shadow boxing to:

1)   Zhang Shanfeng (丰) an itinerant Taoist priest of Mount Wudang in the 15th century around the time of the conquest of the Yuan Dynasty by the Ming Dynasty;

2)   Zhang Shanfeng (峰) an alchemist of Mount Wudang during the reign of Emperor Huizong of the Song Dynasty in the 12th century;

3)   Xu Xuanping, an explorer of mysterious powers in the Tang Dynasty in the middle of the 8th century.

Most of the books on shadow boxing published later than 1921, without research, take Taoist priest Zhang Shangfeng living in the late 15th century as the originator of shadow boxing.

Tang Hao (1897-1959), a martial arts master, and others after research determined in the 1930s that shadow boxing was originated by Chen Wangting

1

of Wen County, Henan province, in the middle of the 17th century when the Ming Dynasty was about to be replaced by the Qing Dynasty. Tang based his judgement on the following evidence:

1) "The 32 Forms of the Canons of Boxing" by Qi Jiguang (1528-1587), which assimilated forms of boxing of 16 schools among folks, makes no mention of shadow boxing;

2) The Five Sets of Shadow Boxing, the One Set of Long Boxing containing 108 forms and the One Set *Paocui* Combat Boxing, created by Chen Wangting of Chenjiangou Village, Wen County, contained 29 of the 32 forms in Qi Jiguang's "Canons of Boxing."

3) Qi Jiguang's "Canons of Boxing" starts with the two forms of "Lazily Belting the Clothes" and "Single Whip," so do the seven set routines of shadow boxing.

4) "The Genealogy of the Chen Families" of Chenjiagou Village has the following explanation under the name of Chen Wangting, their ninth ancestor: "Wangting, alias Zhouting, was a knight at the end of the Ming Dynasty and a scholar in the early years of the Qing Dynasty. Known in Shandong province as a master of martial arts defeating once more than 1,000 'bandits,' was originator of the bare-handed and armed combat boxing of the Chen school. Was a born warrior, as can be proved by the sword he used in combat." (see page 12 of "The Genealogy of the Chen Families")

5) The words of Chen Wangting's "Song of the Canon of Boxing" were copied from Qi Jiguang's "The Canons of Boxing."

6) The first two lines of Chen Wangting's "Song of the Canon of Boxing" — "Changes of actions such as extending and bending are so unexpected as to be totally unpredictable, I rely on all kinds of subtle body movements such as twisting and swirling" — describe the characteristics of the "push hand" techniques of shadow boxing, which are absent in the books on martial arts by such late Ming Dynasty authors as Yu Dayu, Qi Jiguang, Tang Shunzhi and Cheng Chongdou.

7) The Chen families of Chenjiagou Village learned Chen Wangting's boxing routines and "push hand" techniques from generation to generation. After five generations, the shadow boxing of the Chen school was passed on to Chen Changxing (1771-1853), who taught it to Yang Luchan (1799-1872), a native of Yongnian County, Hebei Province. It later developed into shadow boxing of the Yang school, and from which came shadow boxing of the Wu (吳) school in a later period. Wu (武) Yuxiang (1812-1880) of Yonging County learned the original shadow boxing of the Chen school from Yang Luchan and the Zhaobao-style shadow boxing of the Chen school from Chen Qingping, and incorporated the two to create shadow boxing of the Wu (武) school, from which was later developed shadow boxing of the Sun school. These

2

are the well-known five schools of the traditional shadow boxing routines, whose relationship in evolution and development is very clear.

8) As Qi Jiguang died in 1587, shadow boxing can only be a kind of boxing originated later than Qi's "Canons of Boxing;" furthermore, it is one based on the 32 forms contained in Qi's "Canons of Boxing."

The conclusion drawn in the 1930s was that shadow boxing was created around the time when the Ming Dynasty was being replaced by the Qing Dynasty by Chen Wangting of Wen County, Henan Province, a warrior in the late Ming Dynasty.

In the 1960s, following the discovery of more historical data on shadow boxing, the correct time of the origin of shadow boxing was determined to be the 1660s, namely, about 20 years after the overthrow of the Ming Dynasty. The evidence is that, according to "Annals of Huaiqing Prefecture," "Annals of Wen County," and "Annals of Anping County," Chen Wangting was the chief of civil troops defending Wen County three years before the downfall of the Ming Dynasty (1644), who, following Wu Conghui, the county magistrate, led his troops in beating back the assaulting "bandits."

After the downfall of the Ming Dynasty, Chen Wangting, influenced by Taoism, withdrew from society and lived in solitude. This can be seen from the second half of the poem he wrote not long before his death: "Recalling past years, how bravely I fought to wipe out enemy troops, and what risks I went through! All the favours bestowed on me are now in vain! Now old and feeble, I am accompanied only by the book of 'Huang Ting.' Life consists in creating actions of boxing when feeling depressed, doing field work when the season comes, and spending the leisure time teaching disciples and children so that they can be worthy members of the society."

2. The Creative Achievements Made During the Inheritance of Shadow Boxing

As far as existing historical records on martial arts show, Qi Jiguang was an outstanding person in studying and sorting out martial arts among folks, and so was Chen Wangting living a half century later. On the basis of the 32 forms contained in Qi's "Canons of Boxing," Chen created sets of shadow boxing routines. Though it is impossible to verify what he assimilated specifically from boxing of other schools, it can be presumed from the great number of forms in his seven sets of shadow boxing routines that Chen also absorbed many strong points of boxing of many schools existing at the time.

Making a comprehensive survey of the data on martial arts left by Chen Wangting, one can find that Chen made the following contributions to tradi-

3

tional Chinese martial arts in the process of studying and sorting out the martial arts of his time:

1) Combining martial arts with the techniques of *Daoyin* (the concentrated exertion of inner force) and *Tuna* (deep breathing exercises).

China's health-preserving ways of long standing — the technique of *Daoyin*, meant to activate limbs and the trunk through mind-directed exertion of inner force with simultaneous movements of body-bending and back-inclining, and the extending and withdrawing of limbs; and the technique of *Tuna* consisting in deep breathing exercises of the abdomen — are recorded in the writings of such fourth century B.C. authors as Lao Zi, Zhuang Zi, Meng Zi and Qu Yuan. The Six-animal Exercises created by Liu An of the Han Dynasty and the Five-animal Exercises, which was the result of the revision of the former by Hua Tuo, a famous doctor of the late Han Dynasty, were both health-preserving ways using a combination of deep breathing exercises and the imitation of actions of various animals. They later developed into *Qigong* (deep-breathing exercises) and *Neigong* (exercises of inner-force exertion).

Chen Wangting combined the coordinated actions of the hand, the body, eyes and steps of martial arts with the techniques of *Daoyin* and *Tuna*, causing shadow boxing to become a complete system of exercises characterised by anunity of inner and outward power exertion — "practising a breath inwardly, and muscles, bones and the skin outwardly." Thus, in shadow boxing, the boxer's consciousness, breathing and actions are closely connected.

2) Creating spiral-like twining and arc movements, which are each connected with the other, smooth and graceful, tallying very much with the *Jingluo* theory of traditional Chinese medicine (*Jingluo* — main and collateral channels, regarded as a network of passages, through which vital energy circulates and along which the acupuncture points are distributed). Having their source at the internal organs, *Jingluo* are spread throughout the body and limbs. If the vital energy circulates normally through the *Jingluo* and the vital energy in different parts of the *Jingluo* system is in harmony, the person is healthy and will enjoy a long life, and vise versa. Using the *Jingluo* theory, with fighting arts as a means of strengthening outward strength and the techniques of *Daoyin* and *Tuna* as that of strengthening the inner power, shadow boxing has tremendous effects of health preservation.

Shadow boxing contains spiral-like twining actions, alternatively extending and withdrawing, being tight and loose, and firm and soft. The boxer is required to direct the *Qi* (literally "breath", referring to inner vital energy) by mental exertion and to let the *Qi*, which should be concentrated, spread through the whole body. *Qi* is originated from the pubic region and pressed through the whole body by gradually twisting one's body with the waist as

4

an axis. With the twisting of the waist and spine, the two kidney parts are alternatively tightened and loosened, thus allowing the *Qi* to pass through the *Ren* Channel, the *Du* Channel, the *Dai* Channel and the *Chong* Channel. The *Qi* is pressed upward to the tips of the fingers by twisting the arms and wrists, and downward to the toes by twisting the knees and ankles. Having reach the extremities, the *Qi* then returns to the pubic region. Such practice results in strengthened offensive and defensive force of the body and limbs as well as increased explosiveness of such force. In this way, Chen Wangting not only assimilated but also developed the *Jingluo* theory.

3) Creating the two-man push-hand exercises.

Push-hand is a composite practising method in traditional Chinese martial arts. Since ancient times, there had been separate practices of kicking, striking, tumbling, knocking down and catching. The method of tumbling, practised in isolation from striking, had developed in an independent way. The other four methods, though practised in a combined way, had each distinct characteristics. Owing to the fact that the four methods of kicking, striking, knocking down and catching often caused serious injuries when executed in real earnest, their practice had been largely imaginary and symbolic, giving rise to fancy but purposeless methods of execution. Thus, the martial arts, developed painstakingly by masters of older generations, could not be raised to higher levels. This is the reason why a number of famous branches of boxing in ancient China, after being passed on through several generations, lost their original vitality to remain only in name with no one to teach them. Seeing learners degrade *Neijia* Boxing with fancy, purposeless methods, Wang Zhengnan, Huang Baijia's master, who lived in early Qing Dynasty, lamented that "this school (referring to *Neijia* Boxing) is doomed."

The push-hand method created by Chen Wangting consists in two boxers, with hands joined, practising twining and sticking actions to sharpen the sense of touch of the skin and the sensation within the body. Not only did the method incorporate such combat methods as catching, knocking over and striking, it also improved them. Take catching. Chen Wangting's improved method was not limited to catching the enemy's bone joints to overpower him, but was meant to attack the enemy's vital parts, too. Chen's method was very combat efficient at the time, but, owing to the fact that his kicking method easily caused serious injuries, only the knocking-over method was used.

Creation of the push-hand method dispensed with the requirements on ground space, protective gear and special clothes for practising, making Chen's boxing into a kind of sport that can be pursued by two persons at any place and at any time. Thus, to the combat methods in traditional Chinese martial arts (kicking, striking, tumbling, knocking down and catching) was added a new content — pushing. At present the push-hand in shadow boxing is tending to become an item of combat sports.

4) Creating a set of basic routines for spear combat, in which the spear is kept always about the opponent.

The two-man "sticky-spear" practice, which is among the basic exercises of the kind of shadow boxing using long weapons, solves the problem of safe practising without protective gears. In practising the method, the boxer swirls, twines, shoots out and draws back the "sticky spear" as swiftly as wind and in endless cycles. The method provides a simple and easy way for practioners to raise their martial arts skills.

5) Developing boxing theories as contained in Qi Jiguang's "Canons of Boxing" and creating the theories of hiding firmness in softness and executing different moves to deal with changing tactics of the enemy. Chen Wangting's creative achievement in pugilist theory is embodied in the first two lines of his "Song of the Canon of Boxing:" "Actions are so varied and executed in such a way as to be wholly unpredictable to the enemy, and I rely on twining actions and a host of hand-touching movements." Hand-touching movements refer to the mutual pressing of two practioners' arms to develop the ability of quick reaction and gain the technique of "nobody knows me, while I know everybody." Thus, the outward fighting skills were raised to a higher level where "power comes from within" and "inner energy becomes outward power." This has great significance in the history of Chinese martial arts. It also provided training methods and a theoretical basis for such martial arts masters of later generations as Wang Zongyue, Wu Yuxiang and Chen Xing to further develop shadow boxing.

The principle of practising shadow boxing is that the whole body is relaxed with emphasis placed on the exertion of the mind instead of muscles. The process is: from relaxation to softness which, when accumulated, becomes firmness, and then, the firmness changes back to softness, resulting in both softness and firmness, with one complementing the other. It is required that quick actions be both preceded and followed by slow ones, and that slow actions be slower than those executed by others, whereas the quick ones go faster than the fast ones of others. Such emphasis on inner rather than outward force provides a new valuable training method for raising the level of martial arts skills.

Today, shadow boxing has become one of the popular forms of Chinese boxing. It has contributed to improving Chinese people's health and attracted the attention of both sports and medical science circles. The number of people practising shadow boxing abroad is on the rise and shadow boxing is tending to become an international curing and keep-fit sport item. Chen Wangting, by assimilating the essence of a host of boxing forms and bringing forth new ideas, contributed greatly to the creation of a new form of pugilist art — the shadow boxing.

3. The Evolution of Shadow Boxing During the Past 100 Years

Following the introduction of fire arms 100 years ago, the role of boxing skills on the battle field gradually diminished, prompting martial arts masters to reconsider the goal and the direction of the development of martial arts. Practioners of shadow boxing raised the slogan: "What is the ultimate goal of shadow boxing? It is to keep fit and prolong life." (See "Rhymed Formula for Practising 13 Forms," said to be written by Yao Hanchen, Yang Luchan's student, who was a successful candidate in the highest imperial examinations.) Evidently this was the idea initiating the process in which shadow boxing gradually turned into a set of keep-fit exercises from a fighting art.

Another factor causing shadow boxing to change is its difficult sets of routines involving great physical strength, which were unsuitable for even highly skilled martial arts masters in their advanced age.

When the seven sets of boxing routines created by Chen Wangting were passed to Chen Changxing (1771-1853) and Chen Youbeng after five generations, few people in Chenjiagou Village could practise the Long Boxing containing 108 forms and the sets of routines from the second to the fifth of Shadow Boxing (called also the 13 Forms); and boxers in the Chen family were expert only in the first and second sets of shadow boxing routines, and in the skills of push-hand exercises and sticky-spear exercises, both involving two persons. Furthermore, from this time on, the first set of Chen-family shadow boxing developed into two branches — the Old-style and the New-style, and then, from the New-style came Zhaobao-style, to cater to different learners of shadow boxing.

In order to suit keep-fit purposes, Chen Youbeng created the New-style, which is as extended as the Old-style and dispensed with some extremely difficult actions. Chen Qingping, Chen Youbeng's nephew and pupil, also created a form of shadow boxing, which was compact and slow and, when mastered, could be practised with additional cycles. Thus, without changing the routines, the practioner can go from simple to complicated forms to gradually raise his skills. People called this form Zhaobao-style owing to the fact that Chen Qingping lived after marriage in the town of Zhaobao not far from the village of Chenjiagou.

Yang Luchan (1799-1872), who had learned boxing under Chen Changxing, a contemporary of Chen Youbeng, gradually changed the Old-style routines he had learned from his tutor after coming to Beijing to suit shadow boxing to keep-fit purposes. Yang's version was adapted by his third son Yang Jianhou (1839-1917) to become the Middle-style, which, after repeated adaptation by Yang Jianhou's third son Yang Chengfu (1883-1936), became the finalized Big-style. This Big-style, extended and graceful, has become the famous shadow boxing of the Yang school, the most popular form of shadow boxing in China now.

Yang Luchan and his second son Yang Banhou (1837-1892) taught a set of Small-style to Quan You of Manchu nationality, whose son Wu(吴) Jianquan later taught the Small-style to others, hence it was called shadow boxing of the Wu (吴) school, which now is second only to the Yang school in popularity. The Wu school is similar to Yang school in that it is compact, agile, smooth, even in speed, and devoid of leaps and jumps.

Wu(武) Yuxiang (1812-1880) of Yongnian County created the Wu(武) school on the basis of the Old-style of the Chen family he learned from Yang Luchan at about the time of 1851, and the New-style of the Chen family he learned from Chen Qingping in 1852. Shadow boxing of the Wu(武) school is compact, with emphasis on bodywork and the exertion of inner power. It was passed to Sun Lutang (1861-1932) through Li Yiyu (1832-1892) and Hao Weizheng (1849-1920). Sun was proficient in *Xingyi* Boxing and *Eight-diagram* Boxing. Beginning to learn shadow boxing at the age of 51, Sun created a new form by combining the strong points of the three schools. Now called shadow boxing of the Sun school, the new form is similar to shadow boxing of the Yang school in postures, and to *Xingyi* boxing in theory. He wrote a book entitled "The Theory of Shadow Boxing."

The Old-style shadow boxing of the Chen family was brought to Beijing from Chenjiagou Village in October, 1928 by Chen Changxing's great grandson Chen Fake (1887-1957) and taken up by both old people having practised various forms of shadow boxing for many years and young men with physical strength. This Old-style shadow boxing has spread to big cities across China over the recent years.

The various forms of shadow boxing, despite having different characteristics and styles, have the same training principle: execution of relaxed actions to create a state of softness, which is accumulated to produce firmness, creating a state of firmness and softness complementing each other.

The generally acknowledged new routines of traditional shadow boxing are the result of repeated revisions by our predecessors after hard practice and serious study. Therefore, they can suit such different purposes as the keeping of physical fitness and the acquirement of fighting skills as long as a right choice of them is made for different persons and the principle of advancing step by step is adhered to. It can be said that, when structuring traditional shadow boxing, our predecessors took into consideration both its popularization and the raising of practising standards, as reflected in the content and method of teaching of the art. An outstanding feature of shadow boxing, therefore, is its great adaptability.

The New Style of the Chen family, the Zhaobao Style, the Yang Style, the Wu(吴) Style, the Wu(武) Style and the Sun Style — they all resulted from the revision of the First Set of the Chen family's Old Style shadow boxing. Different though in style, they are the same in the structure and order of routines, showing a marked process of evolution.

The vigorous actions such as leaping and stamping in the First Set of the Old Style shadow boxing were discarded in the new forms.

However, the Second Set of the Chen Style, which still contains vigorous and swift actions such as stamping, leaping and dodging, is markedly different in style from other forms of shadow boxing.

Among weapons used in various forms of shadow boxing, the sword and the spear have passed down to the present. Routines involving the use of weapons vary in the degree of sophistication. Furthermore, there are such routines as are adapted from other branches of boxing, with such characteristics of shadow boxing as softness and smoothness. The two-man "Sticky-spear" method, just like the "push-hand" one, is a unique achievement of shadow boxing.

4. The Curative Effects of Shadow Boxing

Around the time of the 1911 Revolution, shadow boxing enjoyed great fame in Beijing owing to its remarkable curative effects. In his poems recording the anecdotes of martial arts masters residing in Beijing at that time, Yang Jizhi (1886-1965) of Xiangtan County writes: "Who knew shadow boxing in the past? It gained popularity after curing Mr. Tang's ailments." "Who could have expected that the boxing art of the Chen family of northern Henan Province was made popular by the Yang family of southern Hebei Province."

It is true that Yang Luchan and his son Yang Banhou, with their masterly shadow boxing skills, contributed to the popularity of shadow boxing in the martial arts circle in Beijing, but the curative effects of shadow boxing were the main factor causing people to think highly of and learn eagerly the pugilist art. The unique training method of shadow boxing was an underlying factor causing it to develop in the direction of curing illness and keeping fit.

The principle for the practising of shodow boxing is "a serene heart plus a concentrated mind," which allows the nerve centre to rest, improving ability to coordinate the functions of the various organs of the body. Relaxation of the whole body, deep and natural breathing, smooth arc-like actions centering on the waist, and a training method aimed at conveying one's inner force to the tips of the limbs by mental exertion — all these result in harmony of the inside and outside body, unimpeded *Jingluo,* blood vessels and lymphatic vessels, and improved functions of the skeleton, the muscle and the digestive system.   Thus, shadow boxing is most suitable for both physical training and physical fitness. As proved by its social application over the past dozens of years, shadow boxing has certain curative effects for such chronic diseases as neurasthenia, neuralgia, high blood pressure, enterogastritis, heart trouble, TB, arthritis, diabetes, emission and internal piles.   Seriously sick persons, however, should be directed by doctors when practising shadow boxing.

5. The Rapid Popularization of Shadow Boxing After Liberation

Since Liberation in 1949, the Party and government have been attaching great importance to the study, systematization and popularization of the country's traditional martial arts, with shadow boxing as a major item. The early 1960s saw the publication of books on shadow boxing of the Chen, Yang, Wu(吴), Wu(武) and Sun schools, which were extensively used in medical treatment and physical training. Newspapers and magazines often carried articles on shadow boxing. Large numbers of professional and amateur shadow boxing teachers were trained. They taught the art in hospitals, schools, government and people's organizations, factories, parks, city neighbourhoods and rural people's communes. On August 1, 1956 was published "Simplified Shadow Boxing," a book compiled by the State Physical Culture and Sports Commission on the basis of the Yang-style shadow boxing. The simplified shadow boxing is made up of 24 sets of actions in 4 groups chosen from the 34 sets totalling 81 actions in the Yang-style shadow boxing, with all the difficult and repeated actions left out. It takes about 20 minutes to practise one round of Yang-style shadow boxing, whereas only five minutes are needed to go through the simplified one. The actions in the latter are arranged in a from-simple-to-sophisticated order to facilitate learning. Books and hanging pictures on the simplified shadow boxing were published for learners, and a film was made on the same theme as a medium of explanation and demonstration. They have helped popularize shadow boxing throughout the country.

In 1957, the State Physical Culture and Sports Commission edited shadow boxing of the Yang school and published an adequately illustrated book on it entitled "The Sport of Shadow Boxing." Containing 88 forms, the book serves as a textbook for practitioners who have mastered the simplified shadow boxing but want to further raise their skill. The year of 1979 yet saw the publication of another book on shadow boxing containing 48 forms, which have assimilated actions from different traditional shadow boxing branches.

Shadow boxing has been contributing to the physical fitness of the Chinese people since Liberation. Different schools of the art all have the need to develop so that the art can suit the needs of different people. Meanwhile, their parallel development can promote mutual assimilation. In inheriting the martial arts legacy, the urgent task now is to continue researching and sorting out different schools of shadow boxing to get their essence and specific training methods.

THE EVOLUTION OF SHADOW BOXING

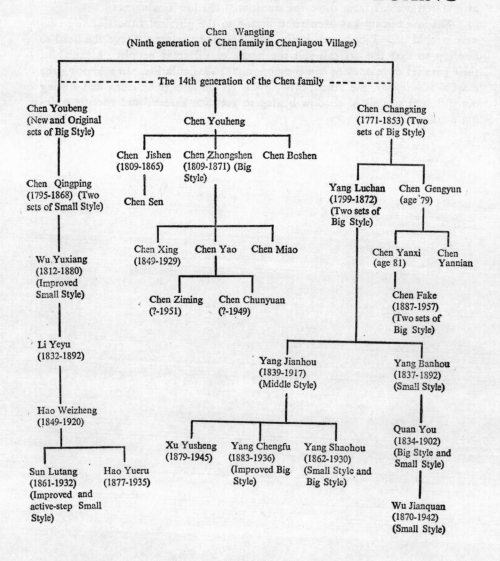

Chen Wangting
(Ninth generation of Chen family in Chenjiagou Village)

------------ The 14th generation of the Chen family ----------

Chen Youbeng
(New and Original
sets of Big Style)

Chen Youheng

Chen Changxing
(1771-1853) (Two
sets of Big Style)

Chen Jishen
(1809-1865)

Chen Zhongshen
(1809-1871) (Big
Style)

Chen Boshen

Chen Qingping
(1795-1868) (Two
sets of Small Style)

Chen Sen

Yang Luchan
(1799-1872)
(Two sets of
Big Style)

Chen Gengyun
(age '79)

Chen Xing
(1849-1929)

Chen Yao

Chen Miao

Wu Yuxiang
(1812-1880)
(Improved
Small Style)

Chen Ziming
(?-1951)

Chen Chunyuan
(?-1949)

Chen Yanxi
(age 81)

Chen
Yannian

Chen Fake
(1887-1957)
(Two sets of
Big Style)

Li Yeyu
(1832-1892)

Yang Jianhou
(1839-1917)
(Middle Style)

Yang Banhou
(1837-1892)
(Small Style)

Hao Weizheng
(1849-1920)

Xu Yusheng
(1879-1945)

Yang Chengfu
(1883-1936)
(Improved Big
Style)

Yang Shaohou
(1862-1930)
(Small Style and
Big Style)

Quan You
(1834-1902)
(Big Style and
Small Style)

Sun Lutang
(1861-1932)
(Improved and
active-step Small
Style)

Hao Yueru
(1877-1935)

Wu Jianquan
(1870-1942)
(Small Style)

Note: Those in squares are representatives of different schools.

12

Part I:

Illustrations of the Attack-Defence Art Series I and II of the Chen-Style *Taijiquan*

Written and Compiled by
Feng Zhiqiang & Feng Dabiao

Performed by
Feng Zhiqiang & Zhang Chundong

Notes About Diagrams of the Attack-Defence Art

1. The contents of this book are not about teaching you how to exercise the Chen-style *Taijiquan*, but about studying how to use the Chen-style *Taijiquan* for attacking and defending, so they are the statements with diagrams of the attack-defence art in Series I and Series II of the Chen-style *Taijiquan*.
2. There are generally A and B in each form of the attack-defence art, sometimes group attack needing A, B and C. No matter what sort of form, A is primary, B and C are secondary.
3. When each form starts, both A and B stand upright with one metre apart.
4. Every diagram of the attack-defence art is divided into two parts — usage and purpose. Some of the usages are coherent and the others seperately belong to several sorts of tricks.
5. All of repeated forms are no longer statemented with diagrams.
6. It should be pointed out that the usage of each form of the attack-defence art is full of variety. An expert is the one who can attack with any part touched by the other party. Statement in words, however, is not able to attend to each and every aspect of a matter: What the book deals with is the most essential usage, but if you keep on exercising, "practice makes perfect", you can grasp the essence from this and "little by little have your own way".

The Names of the Forms in Series I of the Chen-Style Taijiquan

Form 1 Preparing Form

Form 2 Buddha's Warrior Attendant Pounds Mortar

Form 3 Lazy About Tying Coat

Form 4 Six Sealing and Four Closing

Form 5 Single Whip

Form 6 Buddha's Warrior Attendant Pounds Mortar Secondly

Form 7 The White Crane Spreads Its Wings

Form 8 Walk Obliquely and Twist Step on Both Sides

Form 9 The First Closing

Form 10 Wade Forward and Twist Step on Both Sides

Form 11 Walk Obliquely and Twist Step on Both Sides Secondly

Form 12 The Second Closing

Form 13 Wade Forward and Twist Step on Both Sides

Form 14 The Fist of Covering Hand and Arm

Form 15 Buddha's Warrior Attendant Pounds Mortar Thirdly

Form 16 The Punch of Draping Over Body

Form 17 Lean With Back

Form 18 The Blue Dragon Goes Out of Water

Form 19 Push Both Hands

Form 20 Change Palms Three Times

Form 21 The Punch at Elbow's Bottom

Form 22 Step Back and Whirl Arms on Both Sides

Form 23 Step Back and Press Elbow

Form 24 Middle Winding

17

Diagrams of the Attack-Defence Art in Series I of the Chen-Style Taijiquan

Form 1   Preparing Form

Await moving with being quiet. Solid spirit inside and show ease outside without betraying either your feelings or intentions, which gains mastery by striking only after the enemy has struck. If the other party attacks quickly or slowly, you will meet him in the same way.

Form   2   Buddha's Warrior Attendant Pounds Mortar

(Usage 1) If B steps his right leg forward and punches A on his chest with right fist, A gets B's right wrist with right hand, while turns body to the right with waist as axis, right foot parring, left leg Stepping to the rear of B's right shank and sticking. At the same time, A intercepts the outside between B's shoulder and elbow with left hand (*Diagram 1*).

(Purpose) 1. A controls B's shoulder and elbow, so that B cannot step towards him.

2. When B wants to move back and escape, A can hold B's wrist with right hand and beat B's soft rib with left elbow forward. At the same time,

Diagram 1

Diagram 2   Diagram 3

A pulls B's wrist inside while cups the outside of B's elbow in left hand, and holds B's arm straightly (the opposite joint) in such a way as to make B lose any ability of resistance.

(Usage 2) If B removes right leg, A moves B's right hand out towards the left. Meanwhile, A draws an arc downward with right fist to hit B's chin and beat B's crotch with right knee (*Diagram 2*).

(Purpose) 1. Move out B's right hand so as to make B's chest exposed.

2. At the same time, if B resists with left hand, A can control it with left hand.

(Usage 3) While A moves his knee forward, if B inclines body to the right and turn neck so as to shun A's right fist, at the same time, beats A's right knee with left fist, A can take the opportunity to shock with heel to injure the surface of B's left foot (*Diagram 3*).

(Purpose) The structure of the foot-surface bone generally makes up of small pieces. It's easy to be injured by shocking, which makes B lose any ability of resistance.

Form 3   Lazy About Tying Coat

(Usage 1) If B hits A's chest with right hand, A sticks it's right outside with right forearm so as to make B incline to the left. In the same time, A controls B's right upper arm with left hand (*Diagram 4*).

20

Diagram 4

Diagram 5

(Purpose) 1. First makes B incline to the left and lose the centre of weight.
2. Prevents B from taking the opportunity to hit elbow with right arm.

(Usage 2) A takes the opportunity to go downward with right hand to B's right rear, and leans against B's armpit with shoulder, meanwhile A steps right foot to the front of B's crotch (*Diagram 5*).

(Purpose) 1. Makes B continue to incline to the left and prevents B from leaning with shoulder first.

2. Makes B's breath floats up and be not able to keep down so that it is liable to fall outwards.

(Usages 3) If B wants to move back, A again steps right foot forward to tie the outside of B's left foot. (In this time, left foot is ahead.) At the same time, hits B's soft rib by changing shoulder to elbow, which makes B fall outward on a sudden (*Diagram 6*).

(Purpose) 1. Ties B's left foot so as to make B lose balance.

Diagram 6

Diagram 7   Diagram 8

2. Ties below and hit above so as to make the other party impossible to defend effectively.

Form 4 Six Sealing and Four Closing

(Usage 1) If B moves left foot forward and stretches left hand hitting towards A's chest, A first holds B's wrist quickly with left hand (*Diagram 7*). At the same time, turns toes of left foot outward and steps right leg to the rear of B's left leg tying closely (*Diagram 8*). Then, drags B's upper part of elbow with right hand (*Diagram 9*).

(Purpose) 1. Makes B's body incline to the right and weight not keep steady.

2. A holds B's wrist with left hand and drags B's elbow with right hand to catch B's left arm by the holding skill of opposite joint.

Opposite joint means making joint uncomfortable.

(Usage 2) If B resists with the elastic and shaking force, A takes the opportunity to loose hand, sticking B's arm closely and slipping down. Then presses B's left soft rib downward with both hands (*Diagram 10*).

(Purpose) 1. Prevents B from hitting A's upper part with arm and elbow while B leaps and shakes.

2. Makes B's left armpit exposed so as to hit B's rib.

Form 5 Single Whip

22

Diagram 9

Diagram 10

Diagram 11

Diagram 12

(Usage 1)   If B stretches left palm to hit A's chest while left leg is ahead, A quickly moves right leg forward to the outside of B's left foot, clenches the tip of B's four fingers with right hand and holds them forcedly to wring outward (*Diagram 11*). At the same time, stretches left hand to intercept the inside of B's wrist (*Diagram 12*).

23

Diagram 13   Diagram 14

(Purpose) 1. A closes both hands, which makes the opposite joint between fingers and wrist of B's left hand be reduced to inferiority.

2. B cannot escape and loses any ability of resistance.

(Usage 2) If B stretches right hand to hit A's face, A pushes out with left hand (*Diagram 13*), then forms Single Whip. At the same time, steps left foot to the front of B's right foot and draws fingers of right hand while raising wrist to further hold over B's left hand outward (*Diagram 14*).

(Purpose) 1. In the case that B's left hand loses any ability of resistance, B's right hand cannot bring its strength into full play, too.

2. Once the other party is on his back, the weight will certainly not keep steady.

Form 6   Buddha's Warrior Attendant Pounds Mortar Secondly

The usage and purpose are the same as the preceding Form 2.

Form 7   The White Crane Spreads Its Wings

(Usage 1) If B presses A's both arms with both hands and pushes forward forcedly while right foot is ahead (*Diagram 15*), A goes towards B's left rear with right arm down while turning body to the left (*Diagram 16*). At the

24

Diagram 15

Diagram 16

Diagram 17

Diagram 18

same time, sticks the outside of B's right arm with left hand. Then, steps right leg and leans hitting B's chest with right shoulder (*Diagram 17*).

(Purpose) First makes B's both arms come to nothing and the weight cannot keep steady.

2. The fist manual puts, "Lead to coming to nothing and out comes clos-

25

Diagram 19   Diagram 20

ing." In this time, A suddenly hits with shoulder while drawing B to come to nothing and having closed himself, so B falls outward like getting an electric shock.

(Usage 2) If B turns body to the right while his left hand pushes the back of A's right shoulder so as to make A's shoulder come to nothing (*Diagram 18*), in this time, A sticks B's right wrist with left hand and goes under B's right armpit with right hand (*Diagram 19*). Then hits with the back of elbow while turning body to the right (*Diagram 20, the reverse side of Diagram 20*).

(Purpose) 1. Makes the opposite joint of B's right arm be reduced to inferiority.

2. Makes B's left hand be no longer able to bring its strength into fully play.

Form 8   Walk Obliquely and Twist Step
on Both Sides

(Usage 1) If B hits A's chest with right hand while right foot is ahead, A first steps right leg to the front of B's right foot and holds B's right wrist with right hand (*Diagram 21*). Meanwhile, steps left to the outside of B's right leg to stick it (*Diagram 22*). Then presses B's right forearm with left hand and hits B's chest, so B falls outwards at once (*Diagram 23*).

(Purpose) 1. Holds B's right wrist so as to make B's weight incline to the left.

The reverse side of Diagram 20

Diagram 21

Diagram 22

Diagram 23

2. Steps leg to the outside of B's right leg so as to prevent B's right leg from escaping backward.

3. Presses B's right forearm with left hand so as to prevent B's elbow hitting.

4. A sticks B's right leg with left leg and uses hitting skill in the upper

Diagram 24   The reverse side of Diagram 24

part, which makes B be difficult to guard against high and low.

(Usage 2)   When A's left leg steps to the outside of B's right leg, B's right leg cannot escape backward. But if B steps left leg and hits A's chest with left hand, A can take the opportunity to incline body to the left, left hand moving B's left arm out, right hand going to B's soft rib below armpit, and then closing both hands to pull towards the right into Single Whip Form, which makes B fall towards the right rear (*Diagarm 24, the reverse side of Diagram 24*).

(Purpose)   1. B wants to hit A's chest with left hand when moves left foot forward. A takes the opportunity to incline body to the left, which makes B's left hand come to nothing.

2. While B comes to nothing with his weight not keeping steady, A takes the opportunity to move B's right hand with left hand and make it in the opposite joint. In this case, B is not in power. A further goes with right hand to the place below B's right armpit closing and giving strength towards the right rear, so B certainly falls outward.

Form 9   The First Closing

(Usage 2)   If B kicks A's crotch with right foot, A raises left knee to go against B's heel. Meanwhile, A catches B's right foot with both hands (right hand catches the inside of anklebone and left hand catches the outside of

Diagram 25   *Diagram 26*

shank), twining inward forcedly which makes B's right leg be reduced to inferiority of the opposite joint (*Diagram 25*).

(Purpose) 1. A raises left knee to protect his crotch tightly, which makes B be not able to succeed.

2. A goes against B's heel with left knee so as to make B's right leg be not able to fall down, in which there is a holding skill.

3. Makes B stand on only one foot, in this case, the weight doesn't keep steady.

(Usage 2) In this time, if B wants to draw right leg backward, A takes the opportunity to drop left foot closing. Meanwhile, pushes out both hands downward, which makes B fall down (*Diagram 26*).

(Purpose) 1. B stands originally on one foot, A takes the opportunity to exert his strength, which certainly makes B be not able to stand steady.

2. A can bring his strength into fully play only with closing.

Form 10   Wade Forward and Twist Step on Both Sides

(Usage 1) If B moves right foot forward and hits A's chest with right hand (*Diagram 27*). A turns toes of right foot outward and steps left foot to the outside of B's right leg. At the same time, holds B's right wrist with right hand (*Diagram 28*) and draws right arm with left hand, which forms dragging state (*Diagram 29*).

Diagram 27

Diagram 28

Diagram 29

Diagram 30

(Purpose) 1. Makes B incline to the left and the weight not keep steady.
2. Prevent B from hitting elbow.

(Usage 2) If B moves back right hand and foot, A takes the opportunity
to step right leg blocking B's left leg. At the same time, puts right hand under
B's left armpit (*Diagram* 30), then nestles B's chest with right shoulder and hits

Diagram 31   The reverse side of Diagram 31

B's soft rib with right elbow (*Diagram 31, the reverse side of Diagram 31*).

(Purpose) 1. Although B has moved right leg back, his left leg is blocked.

2. A nestles B's chest with shoulder, which makes B be not able to close chest and the breath be liable to float up. The main purpose is still for hitting B's right side of soft rib with elbow.

Form 11   Walk Obliquely and Twist Step
on Both Sides Secondly

The same as the preceding Form 8.

Form 12   The Second Closing

The same as the preceding Form 9.

Form 13   Wade Forward and Twist Step
on Both Sides

The same as the preceding Form 10.

Diagram 32   Diagram 33

Form 14 The Fist of Covering Hand and Arm

(Usage 1) If B hits A's chest with right palm while right foot is ahead, A stretches right hand to hold the opposite joint of the back of B's right hand (*Diagram 32*) pushing out towards the lower part of B's chest, and then places left hand on B's right forearm to form combined strength (*Diagram 33*).

(Purpose) 1. Holds the opposite joint of B's right arm so as to make B lose any ability of resistance.

2. A's both hands form combined strength, which is for stepping up force.

(Usage 2) Follow the previous form, A changes both feet front and back and moves left foot to the outside of B's right foot. In this time, if B wants to free himself from the holding skill by hitting downward A's abdomen (*Diagram 34*), A takes the opportunity to move out B's right arm with left hand by smooth twining, meanwhile, hits B's chest with right fist (*Diagram 35*).

(Purpose) 1. A moves out B's right arm in order to break with vertical strength by horizontal strength, which makes B's chest fully exposed so as to be hit at any parts.

2. This form is called "the Fist of Covering Hand and Arm", just as its name implies, what so called "covering hand and arm" has the meaning of invisible strength so as to make the other party not easy to be found. As it has been found, the other party has fallen outward for ages.

Diagram 34 *Diagram 35*

Form 15　Buddha's Warrior Attendant
Pounds Mortar Thirdly

The slight difference between this Form and the preceding Form 2 is that A first makes B's both hands into opening form, and then kicks with right

Diagram 36 *Diagram 37*

Diagram 38　　　　　　　　　　　*Diagram 39*

foot. Namely, if B steps right foot and pushes A's chest with both palms, A parts B's hands from the inside with both ones, right hand pressing the inside of B's left forearm and left hand moving up B's right wrist backward, which makes B's both hands into high and low opening form (*Diagram 36*). Meanwhile, the inside of A's right foot goes in an arc to close inward the inside of B's right one so as to make B be not able to close high and low and fall forward towards A's right rear (*Diagram 37*).

Form 16　The Punch of Draping Over Body

(Usage 1) If B hits A's chest with right hand (or left hand) (*Diagram 38*), A moves out the inside of B's right forearm from B's left rear with left forearm while both hands clenching fists and curving elbows. At the same time hits the left part of B's face with right fist (*Diagram 39*). If B hits A's chest with left hand, A reverses right hand and left one.

(Purpose) 1. B uses vertical boxing, but horizontal strength breaks with vertical strength, so A uses horizontal boxing to make B's weight slant.

2. While B has no time to hit back with weight slanting and body inclining, A takes the opportunity to hit his face.

(Usage 2) If B hits A's chest with right hand or left one, A turns the state of both hands which clench fists and curving elbows into that of joining strength inward. And if B's right hand is ahead, A can hit the outside of B's

Diagram 40   *Diagram 41*

elbow with left forearm. Meanwhile, hits the inside of B's right wrist with right forearm and inclines body to the right (*Diagram 40*). If B's left hand is ahead, A reverses right hand and left one.

(Purpose) 1. There are both holding skill and hitting skill in it, which makes B's right arm or left one in the state of opposite joint and lose any ability of resistance.

2. While B loses power, A can attack the other party at will.

Form 17   Lean With Back

(Usage) If B moves right foot forward and hits A's chest with right fist, A stretches right hand to hold B's right wrist and turn it over (*Diagram 41*) while stepping left foot to the inside of B's right foot. At the same time, close crotch inward and turns waist with left hand on it, hitting the outside of B's right arm with the inside of left forearm downward towards the right (*Diagram 42*), which makes B's right arm into the state of the opposite joint so that B suddenly falls outward (*Diagram 43*).

(Purpose) 1. There is holding skill in it. If B stretches fist, A holds the wrist; if B stretches palm, A twists it.

2. B's right arm loses any ability of resistance, which is reduced to the inferior position, still less B's left arm.

35

Diagram 42

Diagram 43

Form 18   The Blue Dragon Goes Out of Water

(Usage 1)   If B moves right foot forward and hits B's face with right fist, A hangs left hand on the outside of B's right arm while left foot is ahead

Diagram 44

Diagram 45

Diagram 46   *Diagram 47*

(*Diagarm 44*). At the same time, hits B's right soft rib with the back of left hand (*Diagram 45*).

(Purpose) 1. Hangs on B's right arm so as to make B's body incline.

2. Makes B's right soft rib exposed so as to hit it.

(Usage 2) If B moves right foot back and hits horizontally A's left hand, with right elbow, A quickly steps right foot to the inside of B's left foot and hits B's chest, abdomen and crotch with right shoulder, arm and fist at the same time (*Diagram 46*).

(Purpose) 1. While B removes right elbow to hit horizontally A's left hand, B's chest, abdomen and crotch are all exposed, A can take the opportunity to attack them.

2. Makes B be not able to keep the steady position.

Form 19　Push Both Hands

(Usage) If B moves left foot forward and hits A's chest with left fist, A first holds B's left wrist to the left front with left hand (*Diagram 47*), Mean-while steps right foot to the rear of B's left foot, then hits the part between left shoulder and elbow so that B suddenly falls outward (*Diagram 48*).

(Purpose) 1. A holds B's left wrist with left hand, which makes B first reduced to the inferior position with his left shoulder and rib exposed, at the same time, B's right hand cannot strike back.

Diagram 48　　　　　　　　Diagram 49

2. A steps right foot to the rear of B's left foot so as to make B be not able to move his leg back. On B's raising his leg, A joins forces to attack, which makes B impossible to defend effectively.

Form 20　Change Palms Three Times

This form is the holding skill of the Chen-style *Taijiquan*. There are two usages of it:

(Usage 1) If A first hits B with right hand and his wrist is held by B's left hand (or right hand) (*Diagram 49*), A can then hold the upper part of Be's left wrist (or right wrist) with left hand (*Diagram 50*) while right hand going up forward and turning down. At the same time, while closing chest, both hands join forces to hold the opposite joint of B's wrist, which makes B have to kneel down (*Diagram 51*).

(Purpose) Once one's opposite joint is held, he is in the inferior position. While B kneels down, A takes the opportunity to shake hitting with both hands joining forces. In that case, B is hit outward.

(Usage 2) If B is hitting A's face with right palm, A stretches right hand to hold the ends of B's right fingers (*Diagram 52*) and catches B's right wrist with left hand. At the same time, A steps right foot forward (*Diagram 53*) to make right knee and hand close each other high and low and holds the op-

Diagram 50

Diagram 51

Diagram 52

Diagram 53

posite joint of B's right wrist, which makes B have to kneel down (*Diagram 54*).

(Purpose) Holds the ends of B's fingers, and B's feet are pulled up. In that case, B fully loses any ability of resistance.

Diagram 54   *Diagram 55*

Form 21   The Punch at Elbow's Bottom

This form is the quick spot-hitting skill of the Chen-style *Taijiquan*. It's all right for left, right, or not stepping leg forward.

(Usage) If B hits A's chest with right fist, A makes a false stepping left foot and blocks the outside of B's right elbow joint with left palm towards B's left rear (*Diagram 55*). At the same time, hits A's right rib with right palm (*Diagram 56*).

(Purpose) A blocks the outside of B's right elbow joint with left palm, which makes B's body incline with right rib exposed so as to be casy A's right fist to attack.

Form 22   Step Back and Whirl Arms on Both Sides

(Usage 1) If B moves right foot forward and hits A's chest with right fist, A removes left foot half a step outward and moves out the outside of B's right forearm with right hand from bottom to B's left top. In this time, A can hit B's any parts with left hand at will (*Diagram 57*).

(Purpose) 1. A drags the outside of B's right forearm with right hand, which makes B's attacking strength come to nothing.

2. Makes B's body incline and the right part of his body exposed, so that A has an opportunity to attack at will.

Diagram 56

Diagram 57

3. B's left hand cannot bring power into play.

(Usage 2) If B keeps on attacking by right elbow hitting with continuous steps, A quickly move right foot back with left hand pressing the upper part of B's elbow, and right hand being ready to attack B's face at any time (*Diagram 58*).

(Purpose) Because B comes attacking with tremendous force, A's removing step can play the role which slackens B's efforts, sticks B's elbow and observes B's variations of situation.

Diagram 58

Form 23 Step Back and Press Elbow

(Usage 1) If A attacks first with right foot stepping forward and right fist hitting (*Diagram 59*), unexpectedly, B holds A's right wrist with left hand

Diagram 59   Diagram 60

The reverse side of Diagram 60   Diagram 61

while stepping right leg. A then takes the opportunity to press the back of B's·
left hand firmly (*Diagram 60, the reverse side of Diagram 60*). At the same·
time, twists body inward while turning waist, right elbow pressing the opposite·
joint of B's left elbow, left palm hitting B's face (*Diagram 61*), and right leg
moving back quickly, so that B is forced to fall forward (*Diagarm 62*).

42

Diagram 62   Diagram 63

(Purpose) 1. This is a special holding skill of the Chen-style *Taijiquan*. B holds A's wrist, which outwardly has small advantages but inwardly is taken in.

2. A presses the opposite joint of B's left hand firmly. While B feels unwell, A can hit B's face with right fist. This is so called as the both uses of holding and hitting skill.

(Usage 2) It is all the same conversely and can be used in both right and left style.

Form 24　Middle Winding

(Usage) If A moves right foot forward and hits B's right chest with right fist (*Diagram 63*), B steps right foot and moves B's right fist up with right fist, meanwhile, hits A's right rib with left fist (*Diagram 64*). In this time, A sticks B's right wrist to drag towards the right rear of himself and steps left leg below B's right hip to intercept it, left hand passing below B's right armpit to B's waist, left elbow closing with left knee, which makes B fall backward by Middle Winding Form (*Diagram 65*).

(Purpose) 1. There are two purposes of A's stepping left leg. (1). Shuns B's left fist which is hitting A's right elbow. (2). Intercept B's right leg's retreat.

2. Meanwhile, A can hit B's face with right fist yet.

Diagram 64   *Diagram 65*

Form 25   The White Crane Spreads Its Wings

The same as the preceding Form 7.

Form 26   Walk Obliquely and Twist Step on Both Sides

The same as the preceding Form 8.

Form 27   Flash the Back

(Usage 1) If B moves right foot forward and hits A's chest with left fist, A quickly steps left foot to the inside of B's right foot and presses B's left wrist down with left fist (*Diagram 66*). At the same time, pointed at B's throat with right palm (*Diagram 67*).

(Usage 2) If B's right hand passes by the chest (*Diagram 68*), A can take the opportunity to turn right wrist over with palm facing down to press B's right wrist. At the same time, left foot further inserts to B's crotch while body turns quickly and right foot moves back. Then, hits the outside of B's right shoulder with left elbow erecting, which makes B fall forward suddenly (*Diagram 69*).

44

Diagram 66

Diagram 67

Diagram 68

Diagram 69

(Purpose) 1. This is the special tumbling skill of the Chen-style *Taijiquan*.

2. In Usage 1, it is vertical strength that B is hitting with left hand, so A closes it with pressing strength. In this time, B's throat is exposed, A can take the opportunity to attack.

3. A steps left foot, turns body, moves right foot back quickly and holds

the opposite joint of B's right arm while A's right wrist turns over to press B's right wrist, so B naturally has to fall forward.

Form 28   The Fist of Covering
Hand and Arm

The same as the preceding Form 14.

Form 29   Six Sealing and Four Closing

The same as the preceding Form 4.

Form 30   Single Whip

The same as the preceding Form 5.

Form 31   Wave Hands

(Usage 1)   If B moves right foot forward and hits A's chest with right fist (*Diagram* 70), A inserts left foot to B's crotch while right foot is ahead (If

Diagram 70

Diagram 71

left foot is ahead, right foot moves half a step forward.) At the same time, catches B's right wrist to push aside with right hand and leans against the outside of B's right forearm hitting with left forearm (*Diagram 71*), B falls forward (*Diagram 72*).

(Usage 2) If B moves left foot forward and hits A's chest, A inserts right foot to B's crotch while left foot is ahead (If right foot is ahead, left foot moves half a step forward). At the same time, catches B's left wrist to push aside with left hand and leans against the outside of B's left forearm hitting with right forearm (*Diagrams which are the same as Diagram 70, 71 and 72 but in the opposite direction are omitted*).

(Purpose) 1. A inserts foot to B's crotch, which is for stepping up explosive force.

2. A pushes B's right wrist aside with left hand and takes the opportunity to hit with right forearm, which makes B's left arm straight and the joint of elbow reduced to inferiority. In that case, B has to fall outward.

3. This is the special leaning-holding skill of the Chen-style *Taijiquan*.

Form 32   High Pat on Horse

(Usage 1) If B stretches left palm to hit A's chest while left foot is ahead (*Diagram 73*), A steps right foot to the outside of B's left foot while left foot

Diagram 72   Diagram 73

Diagram 74

is ahead, turning waist and inclining body to the left. At the same time, A holds and drags B's left forearm with left hand, then hits B's left face with right palm (*Diagram* 74).

(Usage 2) If B stretches right palm or kicks both feet, A can change both hands to attack (*Diagram* 75, *the reverse side of Diagram* 75.)

Diagram 75

The reverse side of Diagram 75

(Purpose) 1. A turns waist and inclines body so as to make B's attack come to nothing. Takes B unawares, stays clear of B's main force and strikes at his weak points.

2. A can change with left hand to hold B's wrist and press B's forearm with right hand, making B kneel down by twining-holding skill of holding up and pressing down.

Form 33   Rub With Right Foot

(Usage 1) If B hits A's chest with right foot moving forward and left palm stretching, A steps right foot (*Diagram 76*) to the inside of B's right foot while left foot is ahead. At the same time, right hand presses down B's right forearm from the outside (*Diagram 77*) and left foot inserts behind B's right shank to lock it. Then, left hand hits B's chin, which makes B into the position of falling backward (*Diagram 78*).

(Usage 2) While A steps left foot, if B finds and quickly moves rear leg back, then hits A's chest with left fist (*Diagram 79*), A can push B's left arm upward towards B's right rear with left arm so as to make B's left rib exposed. In this time, if B moves left foot back, A kicks B's left front part with right hand, which forms the skill that pushes high and hits low, stays clear of B's main force and strikes at weak points (*Diagram 80*).

Diagram 76

Diagram 77

Diagram 78   *Diagram 79*

(Purpose) 1. A locks B's leg in order not to make it escape. Meanwhile hits B's chin, add to the special shaking-hitting strength of the Chen-style *Taijiquan*, which can destroy B's cranial nerve.

2. If B is resourceful enough to escape, A can further draw B to expose his left rib, which creates conditions for kicking high and hitting low.

Form 34 Rub With Left Foot

The same as Form 33, except "right" and "left" are reversed.

Form 35 Kick with Left Heel

(Usage) This is the skill of dealing with front or rear enemy at the same time. If A is frontally attacked by B while C hits from the back to help B (*Diagram 81*), A can take them by surprise to incline body and kick C's rib or abdomen with left heel. Meanwhile both fists attack outward, one hitting B and another hitting C (*Diagram 82*).

(Purpose) 1. This is called the skill of looking ahead and behind.

2. A quickly turns body and kicks with left heel, which makes C impossible to defend effectively and have no time to dodge.

3. A's both fists attack outward in the two directions, both hitting B and C.

50

Diagram 80

Diagram 81

Diagram 82

Diagram 83

Form 36   Wade Forward and Twist Step
on Both Sides

The same as the preceding Form 10.

Diagram 84   *Diagram 85*

Form 37   The Punch of Hitting the Ground

(Usage 1) A moves right foot forward and hits B's chest with both hands (*Diagram 83*). It's possible that B takes the opportunity to move right foot back and press B's both shoulders down (*Diagram 84*).

(Usage 2) A can change left hand with fist to push B's rigt chest while taking the opportunity to step left leg. At the same time, A bumps against B's abdomen with head and hits B's left foot with right fist (*Diagram 85*).

(Purpose) 1. A takes the opportunity to attack B with both hands coming to nothing, left fist pushing B's right chest lest B should contain chest and hold down.

2. A attacks B with left fist, head and right fist at the same time, which makes B defend one thing and lose sight of another. In that case, it's difficult for B to parry A's blows.

Form 38   Turn Over Body and Double
Raise Foot

This form is divided into two parts of turning over body and double raise foot.

(Usage 1) Follow the previous form, if A's waist is suddenly hugged by C behind A while A hits B's left foot with right fist, A can immediately draw

Diagram 86   Diagram 87

right shoulder down and then turn it over upward, which forms inertia force of turning over body to hit C with elbow. There are two situations in it, if C doesn't hug A's arms, A can horizontally hit C's right chin with elbow (*Diagram 86, 87*) if C hugs A together with arms, A can horizontally hit C's right soft rib with elbow (*Diagram 88, 89*).

Diagram 88   Diagram 89

Diagram 90   Diagram 91

(Purpose) A holds right shoulder down, which makes C fall towards the right front on account of losing weight and no longer hug firmly, drawing B into the position of coming to nothing. Then vigorously turns over body with elbow hitting so as to make C have no time to escape.

(Usage 2) While A hits B's face with right fist (*Diagram 90*), if B holds down to sweep A's both legs with right leg (*Diagram 91*), A can take the opportunity to bump up by double raising foot and kick B's shoulder, chest or head (*Diagram 92*).

(Purpose) A bumps up by double rising heel, the first, in order to shun B's sweeping leg, and the second, hit B while dodging, which can shoot two hawks with one arrow.

Form 39   Beast's Head Pose

(Usage 1) While A moves right foot forward and hits B's abdomen with both palms, suddenly B presses down A's wrist with both hands (*Diagram 93*) and presses hitting towards A's abdomen forcedly (*Diagram 94*). In that case A immediately moves right foot back with both wrists twining inward (adverse twining) and hits outward, which hits B out (*Diagram 95*).

(Purpose) 1. A moves right foot back, which plays the role of drawing in, so as to make B's force point come to nothing.

Diagram 92

Diagram 93

Diagram 94

Diagram 95

2. A twines inward with both wrists, which makes B's both palms change from smooth to adversity, forming a straight line with both arms. While A hits forward, B falls outward.

(Usage 2) If B moves left foot forward and hits A's chest with left fist, A takes the opportunity to step left foot and draw it out from inside towards

55

Diagram 96   *Diagram 97*

outside (smooth twining) (*Diagram 96*). In this time, if B hits A's chest again with right fist, A can draw it out with left elbow from outside towards inside (adverse twining) and then downward towards B's right. At the same time, hits B's chest or chin with right fist (*Diagram 97*).

(Purpose) Under B's continuous attacking with both fists, A makes B's both fists come to nothing with the twining force which is special in the Chenstyle *Taijiquan and* then takes the opportunity to hit B with right fist.

Form 40　Tornado Foot

(Usage 1) If B moves left foot forward and hits A's chest with left fist, A steps left leg, left hand holding B's left wrist by pushing out, right palm pressing the outside (*Diagram 98*) of B's left shoulder, meanwhile hitting B's left soft rib with right knee (*Diagram 99*).

(Purpose) A holds B's left wrist with left hand pushing out and presses the outside of B's left shoulder with right palm in order to make B's left rib exposed, so as to hit it with right knee.

(Usage 2) If B quickly moves left foot and hand back, then hits A's chest with right fist, A steps right leg, right hand holding B's right wrist and twisting oppositely (*Diagram 100*), left hand holding B's elbow to help right hand, which makes B's right arm into the position of the opposite joint (*Diagram 101*).

(Purpose) It's not easy for B to have the attacking ability of left hand

56

Diagram 98   Diagram 99

while his right arm is in the position of the opposite joint.

(Usage 3) In this time, if B takes the opportunity to move body forward hitting with shoulder in order to free himself from being held (*Diagram 102*), A steps left leg to kick B's right shank by tornado foot from outside towards inside, meanwhile hits left part of B's face with left palm (*Diagram 103*).

Diagram 100   Diagram 101

Diagram 102 *Diagram 103*

(Purpose) It's certainly for B to move shoulder forward by adverse twining hitting A in order to free himself from being held, except which there is no other skill. In this time, the weight of B's right foot must have moved forward. A can take the opportunity to use tornado foot low and blow-on-face palm high hitting at the same time, which makes B attend to one thing and lose sight of another and have to fall backward.

Form 41   Kick With Right Heel

The same as the preceding Form 35, only reversing "right" and "left".

Form 42   The Fist of Covering Hand and Arm

The same as the preceding Form 13.

Form 43   Small Catching and Hitting

(Usage 1) If B moves right leg forward and hits A's chest with right fist, A can steps right leg, right hand holding the tip of B's right hand, left hand pushing the outside of B's right elbow inward, which makes B's right arm into

58

Diagram 104

Diagram 105

the position of opposite joint (*Diagram 104*).

(Purpose) This form is called "Small Catching and Hitting", just as its name implies, there are both catching and hitting in it. This skill is called hand and firmly leans B's right armpit with left forearm (*Diagram 105*), then right palm coordinates left elbow hitting B's right rib (*Diagram 106*).

Diagram 106

Diagram 107

Diagram 108   Diagram 109

(Usage 2) If B takes this chance to hit A's chest with right shoulder, A withdraws right leg and moves left leg forward to hold out against the outside of B's right hip. At the same time A leads B's right hand toward outside of chest with right hand and firmly leans B's right armpit with left forearm (Diagram 105), then right palm helps left elbow to hit B's right rib (Diagram 106).

(Purpose) On the premise of catching-holding, then hits the enemy. A firmly leans B's right armpit with left forearm, which makes B's right rib exposed so as to hit it with right palm or fist.

(Usage 3) If B turns body to the left to escape, A presses B's right shoulder and rib with both palms (*Diagram 107, Diagram 108*).

(Purpose) Hitting with elbow is the attacking skill if short distance. Because B turns body to the left to escape, A's left elbow cannot reach to him. In this time, just as B does not stand steady yet, A hits him with both palms, which naturally makes B fall outward.

Form 44   Cover Head and Push Mountain

(Usage) If B hits A by "Double winds passing through ears", A first draws the insides of B's both hands back with the outsides of both arms with both hands. (*Diagram 109*). Meanwhile, steps right foot to B's crotch by moving a step and hits B's chest with head (*Diagram 110*).

(Purpose) 1. A draws the insides of B's both hands back with the outsides of both forearms. This is the skill of drawing in, which makes B's pounding force come to nothing.

2. A's stepping is named stepping middle part, which makes B frightened and his chest exposed, so as to attack with combined strength.

3. There are four attacking points of this form: both hands, head and foot,

Diagram 110

Form 45   Change Palms Three Times

The same as the preceding Form 20.

Form 46   Six Sealing and Four Closing

The same as the preceding Form 4.

Form 47   Single Whip

The same as the preceding Form 5.

Form 48   Forward Trick

(Usage) If B moves right foot forward and hits A's right face with the back of right hand, A steps right foot to the outside of B's left foot, meanwhile, right hand pushing and pressing the outside of B's right forearm, left hand pushing and pressing the outside of B's right upper arm (*Diagram 111*).

Diagram 111   Diagram 112

In that case, B's body inclines to lose weight, attending to one thing and losing sight of another, and suddenly falls outward (*Diagram 112*).

(Purpose) 1. A's both hands push and press B's right arm at the same time, which makes the right upper part of B's body incline with breath floating up, weight not being steady and right elbow exposed, too.

2. The points to remember of this form: A should pay attention to change both feet, which is done according to B's pace. If B's pace is long, A first moves left foot a step forward, then steps right foot; if B's pace is short, A moves right foot directly. Concerning the position of B's stepping right foot, if to the outside of B's left foot, A can lock B's rear leg; if to the inside of it, A can ram with knee, both of which have the effect of making B fall outward.

Form 49   Backward Trick

(Usage) If B hits the left part of A's face with the back of hand while stepping left foot and stretching left hand, A immediately pulls B's left wrist down with left hand and pulls the upper part of B's left elbow down with right hand (*Diagram 113*). At the same time, steps right foot to the place behind B's left heel and presses the outside of B's left knee with knee (*Diagram 114, the reverse side of Diagram 114*).

(Purpose) 1. A pulls B's left arm down, in which hides the holding skill

Diagram 113

Diagram 114

of opposite joint. B cannot exert his strength with breath floating up. In that case, the left part of B's body loses balance, B's left rib exposed ad his right arm cannot counter.

2.   A presses the outside of B's left knee with right knee, which makes B's left leg into the position of opposite joint and be not able to escape, so B has to fall forward.

The reverse side of Diagram 114

Form 50   Part the Wild Horse's Mane on Both Sides

(Usage 1) If B moves left foot forward and hits A's face with the back of left hand, A first draws the outside of B's left wrist with left hand (*Diagram*

Diagram 115   Diagram 116

115), then steps right foot to the place behind B's left foot, right hand passing below B's armpit, left hand pressing wrist down, and right shoulder raising up, which makes B fall out towards A's front or right (*Diagram 116*).

(Purpose) A draws the outside of B's wrist while B stretches left hand, which makes the left part of B's body into the state of stiffing. In that case, B's right hand cannot naturally bring into play.

(Usage 2) In the series of the Chen-style *Taijiquan*, there are two "Parting the Wild Horse's Mane on Both Sides" in succession. The first one is "Parting the Wild Horse's Mane on Both Sides — Right Style", and the other "Parting the Wild Horse's Mane on Both Sides — Left Style". Both of them has the same usage except that "right" and "left" are reversed (*Diagram 117*).

(Purpose) A presses down B's left wrist with left hand while right knee goes against B's left knee, which makes B's body incline to lose balance. In this time, A can lean hitting with shoulder so as to make B fall backward or forward. It's the same for "Left Style" or "Right Style".

Form 51   Six Sealing and Four Closing

The same as the preceding Form 4.

Form 52   Single Whip

The same as the preceding Form 5.

Diagram 117   Diagram 118

Form 53   Shake Both Feet

(Usage) If B rushes at A's chest with both palms while right foot ahead, A pushes out the inside of B's both wrists from bottom to top with the backs of both hands (right hand is slightly fronter than left one) (*Diagram 118*) while right foot ahead, the fingers of right hand making a false sweep towards B's face. Then A shocks both heels with frightening force and hits down on B's chest with both hands, which uses the "ha" exhaling skill with rib explosive force so that B suddenly falls outward (*Diagram 119*).

(Purpose) 1. A pushes upward with the backs of both hands, which draws B's both palms to come to nothing. In that case, B's breath naturally floats up and the weight is not steady.

2. A makes a false sweep in front of B's face with the fingers of right hand, which makes B's face upward so as to make B's chest exposed.

3. A exhales forcedly ("ha") while shocking with both heels and hitting B's chest with both hands, which is for building up the explosive force. Thus, in a fright, B is in a muddle and cannot protect himself.

Form 54   The Jade Girl Works at Shuttles

(Usage 1) If B moves right foot forward and hits A's chest with right fist, A first pushes out left hand to pull down the inside of B's right wrist, then

Diagram 119   Diagram 120

steps right foot and hits B's chest with right hand (*Diagram 120*).

(Purpose) A pushes out left hand to pull down B's right wrist, which is for turning B's coming force. At the same time of turning, A attacks with right hand.

(Usage 2) If B moves right foot back and presses down A's right hand

Diagram 121   Diagram 122

with left hand (*Diagram 121*), A takes the opportunity to remove right hand down, then goes up to B's throat with left palm (*Diagram 122*).

(Purpose) A removes right hand down, which makes B's left hand's downward pressing come to nothing so as to attack with left hand at the same time. That is what the exposition on *Taijiquan* says, "Drawing in makes the other party come to nothing and there is an attack at once".

(Usage 3) If B moves horizontally A's left forearm with right upper arm (*Diagram 123*) A suddenly turns the toes of left foot inward while turning body backward, right leg making a 180-degree turning backward, right shoulder and elbow hitting the upper part of B's body (*Diagram 124*).

(Purpose) While B moves horizontally A's left hand, A takes the opportunity of inclining to turn body quickly, and takes B by surprise to suddenly hit B on his side.

Form 55 Lazy about Tying Coat

The same as the preceding Form 3.

Form 56 Six Sealing and Four Closing

The same as the preceding Form 4.

Diagram 123

Diagram 124

Form 57　Single Whip

The same as the preceding Form 5.

Form 58　Wave Hands

The same as the preceding Form 31.

Form 59　Shake Foot and Stretch Down

(Usage 1) If B moves right leg forward and stretches right fist to hit A's chest, A draws the outside of B's right wrist with right hand and presses the outside of B's right upper arm with left hand. At the same time, steps left foot to the rear outside of B's right foot (*Diagram 125*).

(Purpose) 1. A draws B's right wrist with right hand, which affects B's tip of the branch so as to attain the goal pulling out B's heels.

2. A presses B's right upper arm with left hand, which makes B's right arm lose any chance of resistance.

3. A's left foot to the rear outside of B's right foot, which makes A himself superior and the other party inferior, meanwhile creates the condition of stepping right leg.

Diagram 125 　　　　　　　　　　　Diagram 126

Diagram 127

Diagram 128

(Usage 2) A quickly steps **right** leg to B's rear crotch with the suddenness of a thunderbolt with left hand pressing B's waist and right hand placing below B's chin (*Diagram 126*). At the same time, A kicks with the rear leg and combines right hand so as to make B incline backward to fall down (*Diagram 127*).

Diagram 129

Diagram 130

(Purpose) 1. A steps right leg, which makes B not be able to escape backward.

2. A presses B's chin down, which makes B not be able to escape forward.

3. A gives out strength at the same time with right foot and hand, building up explosive force by combined strength.

(Usage 3) In this time, if C steps right foot from B's left and attacks with both hands (*Diagram 128*), A draws C's left hand upward with right hand and moves out C's right downward hand, which makes C's both hands separate high and low (*Diagram 129*).

(Purpose) A destroys C's forward join forces of both hands by downward separating force.

(Usage 4) At the same time, A quickly moves down to insert left foot below C's crotch while stepping right foot, and leans hitting C's abdomen with shoulder (*Diagram 130*) to make C fall out (*Diagram 131*). In another skill, A can also shoulder C up and throw him out forward by the elastic — shaking force of shoulder, or throw him out backward by the folding force of shoulder (*Diagram 132*).

(Purpose) C comes violently with both hands attacking, although A breaks with them by the separating force, in order to avoid body's inclining, A takes the opportunity to move down quickly to C's crotch hitting with shoulder by the skill of winning victory in defeat. This skill is rather difficult and the good waist and leg are necessary, so such as practising the form alone or carrying weight on shoulders must be frequently done in normal times.

Diagram 131

Diagram 132

Diagram 133

Diagram 134

Form 60　Stand on One Leg on Both Sides

(Usage 1) If B moves right foot forward and hits A's chest with right fist. A's left hand presses B's right wrist with right foot ahead (*Diagram 133*). At the same time, hits upward B's throat with right fist while stepping left foot to the inside of B's right foot, and raises right knee to dash against B's private parts or abdomen (*Diagam 134*).

(Purpose) 1. A presses B's right wrist with left hand, which creates the condition for raising knee and stretching fist upward.

2.　A steps left foot to the inside of B's right foot, which prevents B from drawing crotch in by turning toes inward, so as to make B form the situation of opportunity to attack B's abdomen or crotch with right knee.

(Usage 2) If B moves right foot back and has escaped from A's right fist and knee, A shocks down with right foot to wound B's left foot (*Diagram 135*).

Diagram 135

This form is "Stand on One Leg — Left Style". It's all the same of usage and purpose for "Stand on One Leg — Right Style" except that "left" and "right" are reversed.

(Purpose) It's said, "Attacking in one's face, one cannot shun the third time." In this form, if B shuns the first (fist) and the second (knee), he cannot shun the third (foot). At last B still loses any ability of resistance.

Form 61   Step Back and Whirl Arms
on Both Sides

The same as the preceding Form 22.

Form 62   Step Back and Press Elbow

The same as the preceding Form 23.

Form 63   Middle Winding

The same as the preceding Form 24.

Form 64   The White Crane Spreads Its Wings

The same as the preceding Form 7.

Form 65   Walk Obliquely and Twist Step
on Both Sides

The same as the preceding Form 8.

Form 66   Flash the Back

The same as the preceding Form 27.

Form 67   The Fist of Covering Hand and Arm

The same as the preceding Form 14.

Form 68   Six Sealing and Four Closing

The same as the preceding Form 4.

Form 69   Single Whip

The same as the preceding Form 5.

Form 70   Wave Hands

The same as the preceding Form 31.

Form 71   High Pat on Horse

The same as the preceding Form 32.

Form 72   Cross Waving Lotus

(Usage 1) If B moves right foot forward and hits A's chest with right fist, A first steps left foot to the outside of B's right leg with about 40 cm

Diagram 136   *Diagram 137*

apart while A's right foot is ahead and left foot is behind. At the same time, stretches left hand to press the joint of B's right elbow from outside towards inside (*Diagram 136*).

(Purpose) 1. In order to shun B's fist, A steps left foot and inclines body to get out of the way.

2. B's right fist comes uprightly, A breaks horizontally with left hand.

(Usage 2) In this time, A's weight moves to the left leg, then steps left leg and raises right knee to the part of B's right rear hip, meanwhile places right hand on B's right hip (*Diagram 137*).

(Purpose) 1. A raises knee to prepare for the next "Cross Waving Lotus".

2. A places right hand on B's right knee and sticks the joint of B's right elbow with elbow in order to prevent B's right hand from changing tricks to hit elbow.

(Usage 3) A's right leg suddenly waves lotus towards the crotch behind B's right leg, right hand pressing on B's waist, meanwhile left hand hitting B's face with the back of palm (*Diagram 138, the reverse side of Diagram 138*).

(Purpose) 1. A attacks high and low at the same time but in the opposite direction with right leg hitting B's lower part of the body by waving lotus and left hand hitting B's upper part in order to pull up B's heels, which makes B fall backward.

2. A's right hand presses B's waist, which helps to pull up B's heels.

Diagram 138   *The reverse side of Diagram 138*

Form 73   The Punch of Hitting Crotch

(Usage 1) If B moves right foot forward and hits A's face with right fist, A steps left foot to the inside of B's right foot. At the same time, A pushes and presses the inside of B's left forearm from inside towards outside with left forearm (*Diagram 139*).

(Purpose) 1. A places left foot to the inside of B's right foot in order not to make B join feet.

2. A pushes and presses B's right forearm outward with right forearm, which makes B's chest exposed.

(Usage 2) If B then hits towards A's abdomen with left fist, A pushes out B's wrist from inside towards outside with right fist by adverse twining. At the same time, takes the opportunity to attack towards B's crotch (*Diagram 140*).

The points to remember in it are twining hip and turning shoulder in order to increase the explosive force.

(Purpose) 1. B's going with left fist is vertical force, while A's pushing out B's wrist is horizontal force. As the saying goes: Horizontal force can break with vertical force.

2. A hits in spirals with right fist while twisting hip and turning shoulder in order to increase the explosive force. There is fist far, there are arm and shoulder leaning to hit near.

Diagram 139

Diagram 140

Diagram 141

Diagram 142

Form 74   The White Ape Presents Fruit

(Usage) If B moves right foot forward and hits A's chest with right fist. A stretches left fist to move B's fist out from inside towards outside while right foot is ahead and left foot is behind. At the same time, raises right knee to hit B's crotch while left foot stepping to the inside of B's right foot (*Diagram 141*) and right foot moving forward, then hits B's chin with right fist (*Diagram 142*).

(Purpose) 1. A moves B's right fist out, which makes B's chest exposed.

2.   A first steps left foot in order not to make B form the combined strength. Meanwhile leans close to B's body, which creates the condition for attacking with right knee and fist.

3.   A raises right knee and fist at the same time, which makes B attend to one thing and lose sight of another.

Form 75   Six Sealing and Four Closing

The same as the preceding Form 4.

Form 76   Single Whip

The same as the preceding Form 5.

Diagram 143   Diagram. 144

Form 77   The Dragon on the Ground

(Usage 2) If B moves right foot forward and stretches right fist to hit A's face, A first sticks the outside of B's right wrist drawing out towards the right with right hand (*Diagram 143*). Then steps left foot to the outside of B's right leg while moving right foot back and draws B's right hand backward (*Diagram 144*).

(Purpose) 1. B comes violently. A takes the opportunity to stick B's strength, which breaks with B's hitting force.

2. It's the method of stealing the beams and pillars and replacing them with rotten timber for A to remove right foot and step left foot. The points to remember in it are turning waist and inclining body, which both avoids B's hitting force and is for drawing B's right hand backward.

3. Makes B's right rib exposed.

(Usage 2) A's right hand sticks B's right hand and not to let it loose. Meanwhile, taking the opportunity to step left foot, hits violently B's right rib with left fist (*Diagram 145*).

(Purpose) 1. What is called soft rib is softer than normal bones, and there are a few free bones which is easy to be wounded.

2. If B moves right hand back, A can take the opportunity to hit B's abdomen.

3. Now that B's right hand is stuck by A, it's not easy for B's left hand to counter.

Diagram 145   Diagram 146

Form 78   Step Forward With Seven Stars

(Usage 1) If B moves right leg forward and hits A's chest with right fist, A stretches right fist to the outside of B's right wrist and pushes it out towards B's left sticking *(Diagram 146)*.

(Purpose) 1. It's vertical strength for B's right fist, and it's horizontal strength for A's right fist to stick the outside of B's wrist and push it out to B's right horizontal strength breaks with vertical strength.

2. In this time, if B does not hit with left fist, A can hit B's right soft rib with left fist.

(Usage 2) In this time, if B again hits A's right chest with left fist, A stretches left fist to the outside of B's left wrist and pushes it out to B's right, which forms Seven Stars posture *(Diagram 147)*.

(Purpose) It's vertical strength for B's left fist to come. A's left fist sticks the outside of B's wrist and pushes it out to B's left, which is still to break with vertical strength by horizontal strength. At the same time, A's both fists form a cross, which calls Seven Stars posture.

(Usage 2) In this time, if A's both hands are quickly catched by B's both palms (B's right hand catching A's right hand, left hand catching A's left hand, both twining adversely towards bosom) *(Diagram 148)*, A takes the opportunity to press on B's abdomen by the combined strength of crossing both palms. If B contains chest and presses down with both hands, A can press

Diagram 147

Diagram 148

Diagram 149

Diagram 150

B's both wrists with both arms while twining adversely with both hands out of bosom from bottom to top, and hit towards B's face with wrist pushing out (*Diagram 149*).

(Purpose) 1. It's easy for B's both hands to be caught inward by B while A's both hands changing for palms. A can only conform to B's force and take the opportunity to hit, which is called the method of pushing the boat along with the current.

2. A conversely intercepts B's both wrists with both arms by the adverse twining method while B pressing down. In this time, A can hit B out by virtue of the forward pushing force of chest and wrist. It's difficult for B to escape from this trick.

Form 79   Step Back and Mount the Tiger

(Usage) If C suddenly steps right foot behind A to hit with both palms (*Diagram 150*) while A wrestles frontally with B, A quickly turns the body to the right and moves right leg to the outside of C's shank under the crotch (*Diagram 151*). At the same time, hits the rear outside of C's right leg with right hip while guiding against B with left palm, and hits the rear of B's right rib with right elbow and forearm (*Diagram 152*).

(Purpose) 1. It's vertical strength for B to rush behind A. A can make him come to nothing by turning the body.

2. A moves right leg to the outside of C's shank under the crotch and leans against C's body firmly, which makes C be not easy to escape.

Diagram 151

Diagram 152

80

Diagram 153   Diagram 154

Form 80   Turn Body and Double Wave Lotus

(Usage 1) If B steps right leg and hits towards A's chest with right fist, A moves right foot forward and presses the right outside of B's forearm towards the right front with left hand. At the same time, A horizontally cuts the ear part of B's left face with right palm, which forms crisscrossing combined strength (*Diagram 153*).

(Purpose) 1. This form is a transition form between "Step Back and Mount the Tiger" and "Turn Body and Double Wave Lotus".

2. A's left hand presses the right outside of B's forearm, which is to break wth vertical strength by horizontal strength.

3. A horizontally cuts the ear nerve of B's left face. In that case, B loses any ability of resistance for the time being.

(Usage 2) In this time, suddenly C steps right foot behind A and hits with right fist (*Diagram 154*). A steps left foot with a 180-degree turning to the outside of C's right leg while quickly twining the body. At the same time, A pushes B's right arm with both hands (left hand pushing shoulder, right hand pushing forearm) (*Diagram 155*).

(Purpose) A goes to the rear outside of C's body while making a 180-degree turning, so A both escapes from C's fist and sticks C's right arm. In

Diagram 155   Diagram 156

that case, C's right arm dare not move back and left arm cannot bring power into play.

(Usage 3) Follow the previous Usage 2, A raises right leg quickly and violently to insert under the rear of C's crotch and gives out force backward. At the same time, A violently hits backward the part between C's front chest and throat with right arm while left hand providing against C's right shoulder (*Diagram 156*).

(Purpose) A puts forth his strength high and low but in the opposite direction with right leg and hard while turning the body, which pulls up C's root of feet low and gives out force high backward. In that case, C cannot but fall backward.

Form 81   The Cannon Right Overhead

(Usage) If B moves right leg forward and hits A's abdomen with right fist, A immediately steps left foot to the outside of B's right foot. Meanwhile A's both fists hang down (*Diagram 157*), twining smoothly to push out from front to bottom, then to top, and then towards outside, left fist hitting B's chin and right fist hitting B's chest (*Diagram 158*).

(Purpose) 1. B's both fists hang down, which is for breaking with B's coming fist by vertical strength.

2. A's both fists twine smoothly to push out from front to bottom, then

| Diagram 157 | Diagram 158 |

to top, and then towards outside, which is for building up the hitting force.

3. This form is similar to Cannon Boxing in *Xingyiquan*. There is only an action more that hangs down and twines smoothly.

Form 82 Buddha's Warrior Attendant Pounds Mortar

The same as the preceding Form 2.

Form 83 Closing Form

The same as the preceding Form 1.

The Names of the Forms in Series II of the Chen-Style Taijiquan

Form 1 Preparing Form

Form 2 Buddha's Warrior Attendant Pounds Mortar

Form 3 Lazy About Tying Coat

Form 4 Six Sealing and Four Closing

Form 5 Single Whip

Form 6 Move and Hinder With Elbow

Form 7 The Fist of Protecting Heart

Form 8 Twist Step on Both Sides and Walk Obliquely

Form 9 Sink Waist With Elbow Down

Form 10 Go Straight With Left palm Into Well

Form 11 Plum Blossoms Scattered by the Wind

Form 12 Buddha's Warrior Attendant Pounds Mortar

Form 13 The Fist of Protecting Body

Form 14 The Fist of Putting Fists Aside Before Body

Form 15 Cut Hand

Form 16 Turn Flowers Out and Brandish Sleeves

Form 17 The Fist of Covering Hand and Arm

Form 18 Jump a Step and Twist Elbow

Form 19 Wave Hands (the Former Three Times)

Form 20 High Pat on Horse

Form 21 Wave Hands (the Latter Three Times)

Form 22 High Pat on Horse

Form 23 Cannons in Series (1)

Diagrams of the Attack-Defence Art in Series II of the Chen-Style Taijiquan

Form 1   Preparing Form

The usage and purpose are the same as those of Form 1 in Series I.

Form 2   Buddha's Warrior Attendant
Pounds Mortar

The usage and purpose are the same as those of Form 2 in Series I.

Form 3   Lazy About Tying Coat

The usage and purpose are the same as those of Form 3 in Series I.

Form 4   Six Sealing and Four Closing

The usage and purpose are the same as those of Form 4 in Series I.

Form 5   Single Whip

The usage and purpose are the same as those of Form 5 in Series I.

Diagram 1   Diagram 2

Form 6   Move and Hinder With Elbow

(Usage 1) If B moves right foot forward and hits A's face with right fist, A first blocks the inside of B's right wrist with right fist. (*Diagram 1*)

(Purpose) 1. It is vertical strength for B's right fist, and it is horizontal strength for A's blocking it with right fist. Horizontal strength breaks with vertical strength.

2. A blocks B's right fist out with right fist by the special twining force of the Chen-style *Taijiquan,* which creates conditions for neat stepping leg and hitting with elbow.

(Usage 2) A's right fist sticks tightly to the inside of B's right wrist drawing B's fist out by adverse twining first upward then downward. At the same time, takes the opportunity to step left foot to the rear of B's right foot, left elbow conforming to B's elbow downward to hit B's soft rib and chest, and left fist hitting B's chin. (*Diagram 2*)

(Purpose) 1. This is the wrestling-hitting skill. If A does not want to B's right foot, which makes B not easy to escape.

2. A's left fist hits B's chin while left elbow hitting B's soft rib and chest, which makes B attend to one thing and lose sight of another.

(Usage 3) This is an attacking skill for A to hit B's soft rib, chest and chin with left elbow and fist. Furthermore, A can yet use the combined strength of left shoulder and left leg at the same time to make B fall outward.

Diagram 3   Diagram 4

(*Diagram 3*).

(Purpose) 1. This is the wrestling-hitting skill. If A dose not want to wound B, A can again use left shoulder and elbow twining outward while left leg blocking B's right leg under the situation of B's having lost weight, which makes B fall backward.

2. This is the hitting skill of "Move and Hinder With Elbow-left Style". The usage and purpose of "Move and Hinder With Elbow-right Style" are all the same, only reversing right and left.

(Usage 4) Another hitting skill, if A hits B's armpit with left elbow, A's right hand attacks B's soft rib by the Fist of Moving and Hindering. (*Diagram 4*)

(Purpose) 1. B's left arm is above and breath has floated up. This hitting skill can block B's breath.

2. This hitting skill forces B's left arm not to be able to return a blow, and B's right arm has no time to counter-attack, too.

Form 7   The Fist of Protecting Heart

(Usage) If C attacks with right fist and leg from A's rear or left side while A wrestles frontally with B (*Diagram 5*), A quickly turns waist to jump up 90 degrees to 180 degrees (*Diagram 6*), and then falls to the ground with right foot ahead and left foot behind. At the same time, A moves C's right fist

Diagram 5   *Diagram 6*

outward with left fist and hits C's chest with right fist. (*Diagram* 7).

 (Purpose) 1. A turns waist to jump up 90 degrees to 180 degrees with the suddenness of a thunderbolt, which is for shunning the attack of C's leg.

 2. A takes the opportunity to move C's fist outward with left hand while

Diagram 7   *Diagram 8*

Diagram 9   Diagram 10

falling to the ground, in order to create conditions for attacking C's chest with right fist.

Form 8   Twist Step on Both Sides and Walk Obliquely

(Usage 1) If B moves right foot forward and hit A's abdomen with right fist, A pushes B's right fist outward with right hand by adverse twining while right foot ahead (*Diagram 8*). At the same time, A moves right leg back (*Diagram 9*) and steps left leg to insert to the rear of B's right heel, then moves left arm to press the inside of B's right upper arm with left elbow (*Diagram 10*), in that case, makes B fall outward by squeezing skill. (*Diagram 11*)

(Purpose) 1. A pushes B's right hand outward with right hand, which makes B reduced to inferiority.

2. A steps left leg to insert to the rear of B's right heel, which is for blocking the retreat of B's leg.

3. A's left elbow presses the inside of B's right upper arm, which makes B's right arm not be able to raise and lose any ability of resistance so as to use squeezing skill.

(Usage 2) If A does not use squeezing skill, A can swing wrist to hit B's face with the back of left hand. Meanwhile, strikes the palm of B's left hand with right palm. (*Diagram 12*)

Diagram 11

Diagram 12

(Purpose) 1. A strikes the palm of B's left hand with right palm to step up the shocking force, which will make it easy for B to suffer from cerebral concussion.

2. A's left leg has blocked B's right leg, so B falls backward himself.

Diagram 13

Form 9　Sink Waist With Elbow Down

(Usage 1) If B moves right foot forward and hits A's face with right hand by the Palm of Rushing at Face, A quickly steps left leg to the front of B's right leg, meanwhile, left palm pressing the outside of B's right elbow. (*Diagram 13*)

(*Purpose*) A sreps left leg in order to shun the hitting opint of B's force, and left palm presses the outside of B's right elbow so as to divert B's attention.

Diagram 14

The reverse side of Diagram 14

(Usage 2) Follow above, A's leg follow closely to insert to the inside of B's right leg, meanwhile, right shoulder sticking to the outside of B's right shoulder (*Diagram 14, the reverse side of Diagram 14*), right elbow hitting the lower part of B's rear soft rib, which makes B fall forward. (*Diagram 15, the reverse side of Diagram 15*).

Diagram 15

The reverse side of Diagram 15

Diagram 16   Diagram 17

(Purpose) In order to hit the rear part of B's right rib with elbow, A first steps right leg to block B's right foot so as to make B not able to retreat, but going forward, B will fall. Elbow above and foot below, B cannot escape.

Form 10   Go Straight With Left Palm Into Well

(Usage 1) If B moves right foot forward and hits A's right chest, A first holds B's right wrist with right hand by smooth twining while right foot ahead. (*Diagram 16*)

(Purpose) It is vertical strength for B's fist coming straight, and A holds wrist by smooth twining to break with it by twining strength of the Chenstyle *Taijiquan*, which makes B's body incline and be reduced to falling forward.

(Usage 2) Follow above, A then steps left leg to insert to the front of B's right foot and dashes against B's right knee with the rear part of shank. Meanwhile hits the lower part of B's abdomen with left palm. (*Diagram 17, 18*)

(Purpose) 1. A's left leg inserts to the front of B's right foot and dashes against B's right knee, which makes B's crotch open outward and not able to form combined strength.

2.   In this time, B's abdomen has been exposed, which creates conditions for A's right fist hitting.

94

Diagram 18

Diagram 19

Diagram 20

Diagram 21

Form 11   Plum Blossoms Scattered by the Wind

(Usage 1) If C hugs A's waist from A's rear while A is wrestling with B (*Diagram 19*), A quickly turns body to hit C's right ear, the right part of neck and hindbrain. (*Diagram 20*)

(Purpose) A suddenly turns body to hit C's right ear, the right part of neck and hindbrain while C hugging his waist, which makes C suffer from pain so that C's body inclines and cannot hug A.

(Usage 2) A continues to press C's neck after hitting C with right elbow. If C quickly slips free towards A's chest, A can immediately hit the right part of C's face with left hand by the Posture of Hitting Ear with One Palm. (*Diagram 21*)

(Purpose) It is like sweeping the ground that A's right arm continues to press C's neck, and C naturally wants to bow his head to escape. In this time, A can just hit the right part of C's face with left palm.

Form 12   Buddha's Warrior Attendant
Pounds Mortar

The usage and purpose are the same as those of Form 2 in Series I.

Form 13   The Fist of Protecting Body

The usage and purpose are the same as those of Form 16 "The Punch of Draping Over Body" in Series I.

Form 14   The Fist of Putting Fists Aside
Befoer Body

(Usage) If B moves right foot forward and pounds A's face from above to below. A stretches right hand outward to block the inside of B's right wrist while right foot ahead (*Diagram 22*). At the same time, moves right foot back and steps left foot to the inside of B's right leg, right fist sticking B's right fist by adverse twining into smooth twining to draw out towards the right, and left fist under B's right elbow hitting towards the left part of B's face. (*Diagram 23*)

(Purpose) 1. It is vertical strength for B's right fist to pound the right part of A's face from above to below, and it is horizontal strength for A's right hand to stretch outward to block B's right wrist. As stated above, horizontal strength breaks with vertical strength.

2.   It is the skill of sneaking attack that A's left fist under B's right elbow hits towards the left part of B's face. B is blocked by his own right arm, so cannot guard against it.

3.   If B uses palm, A can hold his wrist.

Diagram 22   *Diagram* 23

Form 15   Cut Hand

(Usage) If C suddenly hits A's waist with fist or palm from A's rear while A wrestling with B (*Diagram 24*), A quickly turns body to the left, right leg raising knee and stepping forward to shock with foot, left palm upward, right fist downward, hitting C's right wrist by join forces. (*Diagram 25*)

Diagram 24   *Diagram* 25

(Purpose) Wrist is the turning part of joint. A cuts C's coming hand with both hands by join forces, which makes C immediately lose the fighting ability, just as "the Cannon of Cutting Hand" in "Series of Advancing and Retreating" of *Xinyiquan*.

Diagram 26

Diagram 27

Diagram 28

Diagram 29

Form 16   Turn Flowers Out and Brandish Sleeves

(Usage) If C suddenly sweeps horizontally A's ankle with leg from A's rear while A wrestling with B (*Diagram 26*), A quickly jumps up (*Diagram 27*) and turns body 180 degrees in the air (*Diagram 28*), right hand splitting C's right ear, left forearm pounding C's right shoulder. (*Diagram 29*)

(Purpose) 1. A jumps up in order to shun the horizontal sweeping of C's leg.

2. A escapes from the sweeping of C's leg and turns body in the air, which can step up strength through twisting waits in order to hit C with both palms.

Form 17   The Fist of Covering Hand and Arm

The usage and purpose are the same as those of Form 14 in Series I.

Form 18   Jump a Step and Twist Elbow

(Usage 1) A deals with B and C, forming the position of triangle. If B first moves right foot forward and hits A's chest with right fist, A quickly meets the inside of B's forearm head-on with left fist from inside to outside. (*Diagram 30*)

(Purpose) 1. This is the group fighting skill. It is vertical strength for B's right fist to come hitting, so A can break with it by meeting from inside to outside with left fist.

(Purpose) 1. A jumps up in order to shun the horizontal sweeping of C's

(Usage 2) Follow above, in this time if C moves right foot and hits A's left soft rib with right fist, A stretches right fist to make a false hitting towards B while turning body 90 degrees to the left, right foot stepping to the front of C's crotch and right fist turning to hit towards C. (*Diagram 31*)

(Purpose) 1. It is an empty strike that A stretches right fist to make a false hitting towards B. In fact, A takes an advantage of turning body and his objective is C.

2. While A turns body 90 degrees to the left, if B does not pull A's right arm, A's right shoulder can also play the role of blocking; if B pulls it, A is still smoother.

3. A's turning shuns the attack of C's right fist, too.

(Usage 3) While A hits C with right fist, if B moves right leg back and

Diagram 30

Diagram 31

attacks again towards B's back with left fist (*Diagram 32*), A suddenly turns body to the left and moves left foot to the front of B's crotch, at the same time, left hand blocking B's left hand (*Diagram 33*), right arm bending, and right elbow hitting the part between B's left rib and waist with treading steps.

Diagram 32

Diagram 33

(Diagram 34)

(Purpose) 1. It is unexpected to B that A suddenly turns body.

2. A breaks B's left fist with right fist while turning body, which is also that horizontal strength breaks vertical strength.

3. In this time, B is reduced to inferiority. A can quickly hit the part between B's left rib and waist with right elbow.

Diagram 34

Form 19   Wave Hands (the Former Three Times)

The Usage and purpose are the same as those of Form 31 in Series I.

Form 20   High Pat on Horse

The usage and purpose are the same as those of Form 32 in Series I.

Form 21   Wave Hands (the Latter Three Times)

The usage and purpose are the same as those of Form 31 in Series I.

Form 22   High Pat on Horse

The usage and purpose are the same as those of Form 32 in Series I.

Form 23   Cannons in Series (1)

(Usage 1) If B moves right foot forward and cuts horizontally the left

101

Diagram 35   Diagram 36

part of A's face with right palm, A raises both hands at the same time while right foot ahead, left hand pushing the inside of B's right wrist outward, right hand hitting B's chin from below to above. (*Diagram 35*)

(Purpose) 1. A's left hand pushes B's right wrist outward while B's right hand hitting the left part of A's face, which makes B's right rib exposed.

2. A's right hand hits B's chin from below to above, which firstly, stems B's visual line, secondly, makes B's face upward and chest exposed.

(Usage 2). In this time, A quickly steps right foot to insert into the place below B's crotch, meanwhile, both palms hitting violently B's soft rib, chest and abdomen, which makes B fall backward. (*Diagram 36*)

(Purpose) 1. A inserts foot and hits violently with both palms at the same time in order to build up explosive force, which plays the role of pulling up B's heels.

2. If B shrinks abdomen and presses downward while A's both palms hitting B's chest and abdomen, A can take the opportunity to hit B out with shoulder leaning.

Form 24   Cannons in Series (2)

The usage and purpose are the same as those of the preceding Form 23.

Form 25   Cannons in Series (3)

The usage and purpose are the same as those of the preceding Form 23.

Form 26   Ride the Animal in the Reverse Direction

(Usage 1) If B moves right foot and rushes at A's chest with both palms (*Diagram 37*), A takes the opportunity to part B's wrists towards both sides with hands from below to above while right foot ahead (*Diagram 38*). At the same time, catches the tips of B's both hands while turning body to the right, and respectively twists inward to cross before chest (left hand above, right hand below). (*Diagram 39*)

(Purpose) 1. A parts B's both palms with hands in order to make B's breath not able to sink down, which can break with his combined strength and create conditions for catching the tips of B's fingers.

2. A catches the tips of B's hands, crossing before chest, and twists them downward by join forces, which makes B's opposite joint suffer from pains so as to lose any ability of resistance, and forces B to have to bend waist and bow head.

(Usage 2) A quickly looses hands and parts palms back and forth while

Diagram 37

Diagram 38

Diagram 39　　　　　　　　　*Diagram 40*

B bending waist and bowing head, left palm being ahead to hit B's face. At the same time, kicks B's abdomen with left foot to make B fall backward. (*Diagram 40*)

(Purpose) 1. There are three purposes of A's parting palms back and forth: The first is that left palm can hit forward B's face; the second is that it can play the role of balance; the third is that if C attacks from the rear, A can also look ahead and behind to repulse at any time by the skill of "Ride the Animal in the Reverse Direction".

2. There is A's left palm to hit B's face above, and there is A's left foot to kick B's abdomen below. B cannot give attention to both above and below, and is not easy to keep balance.

Form 27　The White Snake Spits Its Tongue (1)

(Usage) If B moves right foot and hits A's chest with right fist, A quickly steps left foot and presses B's forearm and wrist from above to below with left palm (*Diagram 41*), meanwhile, right foot moving a step, right palm facing upward and going horizontally to hit B's throat (*Diagram 42*). In this time, A's right knee can ram B's crotch, too. (*Diagram 43*)

(Purpose). 1. It is vertical strength that B's right fist hits A, and it is pressing strength that A's left palm presses from above to below, which can break with B's vertical strength.

Diagram 41

Diagram 42

2. A steps right leg and stretches right palm horizontally at the same time, which can build up explosive force.

3. A's right palm marches in spirals, which makes B not easy to block it.

4. A's right palm can also change into fist for using.

5. A uses palm above and knee below, attacking up and down, hitting two points at the same time, which makes B not give attention to both above and below.

right foot not able to escape.

Diagram 43

Form 28 The White Snake Spits Its Tongue (2)

The usage and purpose are the same as those of the preceding Form 27.

Form 29   The White Snake Spits Its Tongue (3)

The usage and purpose are the same as those of the preceding Form 27.

Form 30   Turn Flowers Out From the Bottom of the Sea

(Usage 1) A wrestles with B frontally. If B moves right leg forward and hits A's face with right fist, A blocks the inside of B's right wrist with left hand. At the same time, steps left foot to the rear of B's right foot hindering, and hits violently towards B's chest with right fist. (*Diagram 44*)

(Purpose) 1. A steps left foot to block B's right foot, which makes B's right foot not able to escape.

2. A's left fist blocks the inside of B's right wrist, which makes B's chest exposed so that A's right fist attacks.

3. The three points of A's left hand, left foot and right fist go forth at the same time, which is difficult for B to resist.

(Usage 2) In this time, if C suddenly hugs A's waist from A's rear with both hands below A's armpits (*Diagram 45*), A quickly twists hip and waist rises from below to above, which makes C form the shape of falling forward (*Diagram 46*). Then takes the opportunity to hit C's neck with right elbow and ram C's abdomen with right knee. (*Diagram 47*)

Diagram 44

Diagram 45

Diagram 46   Diagram 47

(Purpose) 1. While C hugs A's waist below armpits from A's rear, A turns body to join forces up and down. C has been not able to get up because his neck is hit by A's right elbow, his abdomen is again attacked by A's knee, which certainly makes B unexpected.

2. This is the close hitting skill. Generally speaking, it is difficult for other party to provide against the elbow of turning body and the knee of turning body.

Form 31   The Fist of Covering Hand and Arm

The usage and purpose are the same as those of Form 14 in Series I.

Form 32   Turn Body With Six Closing

(Usage 1) If C suddenly hugs A's both arms and waist from A's rear at the same time, A crosses both hands before abdomen, left hand above, right hand below, and body sinking down. (*Diagram 48*)

(Purpose) 1. A crosses both hands before abdomen with body sinking down. In that case, B's both hands do not hug tightly any longer.

2. This strike makes B expose intervals under B's armpit and at B's soft rib.

107

Diagram 48   Diagram 49

(Usage 2) Follow above, A's right fist stick tightly the part under B's right elbow, forming heading force. At the same time, A's right elbow hits B's right soft rib. (*Diagram 49*)

(Purpose) A's left fist heads B's right elbow, which firstly makes the interval of B's right armpit build up, secondly makes B's breath not able to sink down, so that creates conditions for right elbow to hit B's soft rib.

(Usage 3) A's right elbow hits B's right soft rib, and B suffers from pains to remove body backward. In this time, A can take the opportunity to turn 180 degrees towards right rear and violently shock B's left instep with right foot. (*Diagram 50*)

(Purpose) It is unexpected to B that A can shock his left instep with right foot while B's right rib is hit by A's elbow and suffers from pains to remove quickly. A attacks continuously by elbow hitting and foot trampling.

Form 33   Wrap Crackers — Left Style (1)

(Usage 1) If B moves right foot and hits the right part of A's face with the back of right hand, A quickly pushes the outside of B's right forearm outward with left palm. (*Diagram 51*)

(Purpose) 1. A's left palm pushes the outside of B's right forearm while the back of B's right hand hitting the right part of A's face, which makes B's weight incline.

108

Diagram 50   Diagram 51

Diagram 52   Diagram 53

   2.   It creates conditions for A's next moving shoulder forward.

   (Usage 2) Follow above, A steps right leg to the outside of B's left foot (*Diagram* 52). Meanwhile, hits the right part of B's back with right elbow by the force of parting towards both sides, making B fall forward. (*Diagram* 53)

   (Purpose). 1. A steps right leg to the outside of B's left foot so as to block

B's both feet and make them not able to escape.

2. In this time, there is A's left foot in front of B's foot and A's right elbow behind, left foot low, right elbow high, so B cannot but fall forward.

Form 34   Wrap Crackers — Left Style (2)

The usage and purpose are the same as those of the preceding Form 33.

Form 35   Wrap Crackers — Right Style (1)

The usage and purpose are the same as those of the preceding Form 33, only in the opposite direction.

Form 36   Wrap Crackers — Right Style (2)

The usage and purpose are the same as those of the preceding Form 33, only in the opposite direction.

Form 37   Beast's Head Pose

The usage and purpose are the same as those of Form 39 in Series I.

Form 38   Splitting Pose

(Usage) If B moves right foot and hits the right part of A's chest, A blocks the outside of B's right forearm with right fist (*Diagram 54*), and steps left leg to the rear of B's right foot (*Diagram 55*). In this time, A changes right fist for palm to hold B's right wrist and his left hand and foot forms combined strength, left forearm going through under B's right armpit to hit B's face violently. (*Diagram 56*)

(Purpose) 1. A's right fist blocks the outside of B's right forearm, which makes B's right rib so as to create conditions for next A's palm going.

2. A steps left leg to the rear of B's right foot in order to provide against B's right leg escaping backward.

3. It is called sneaking hand that A's left forearm goes through under B's right armpit to hit B's face, which makes B unexpected.

Diagram 54

Diagram 55

Diagram 56

Diagram 57

Form 39   Turn Flowers Out and Brandish Sleeves

(Usage)   Follow the previous Form, if B moves out A's left arm and removes right leg backward (*Diagram 57, 58*), A jumps up with legs back and forth changing their positions in the air (*Diagram 59*), and splits down with

111

Diagram 58

Diagram 59

Diagram 60

Diagram 61

both hands just like swinging a hammer to forge iron: right hand splitting B's left ear or the left part of neck, right hand splitting B's left forearm. (*Diagram 60*)

(Purpose) 1. B certainly holds A's left foot while removing right leg, so A jumps up to change both leg's positions, which is called the skill of steeling

| Diagram 62 | Diagram 63 |

the beams and pillars and replacing them with rotten timber.

2. B frightens with face upward and wants to protect his chest while A's left hand splitting down, so it is just the time that A takes the opportunity to split B's left ear or the left part of neck with right hand.

Form 40   The Fist of Covering Hand and Arm

The usage and purpose are the same as those of Form 14 in Series I.

Form 41   Tame the Tiger

(Usage 1)   If A's left leg is hugged by B's both hands (*Diagram 61*), A quickly turns weight to the right, left forearm holding the back of B's neck, right fist hitting B's hindbrain. (*Diagram 62*)

(Purpose)   1. A turns weight to the right, which can cause B's weight to fall forward. In that case, it is difficult for B to hug A's left leg tightly.

2. A's left forearm holds the back of B's neck in order not to let him escape.

3. (The Song of *Taijiquan* Pushing) puts, "A palm hitting the hindbrain is a mortal one", so it can be seen that hindbrain is the vital part of a person.

(Usage 2)   For previous form, A has another defeating skill. Namely,

113

A's left hand does not hold the back of B's neck. At the same time, hits B's hindbrain with right fist. (*Diagram 63*)

(Purpose) 1. A's left hand inserts downward from the right outside of B's neck, which makes B's head incline. In that case, it is difficult for B to continue to hug A's left leg tightly.

2. In this time, A can hit any part of B's head at will.

Form 42　The Hitting of Rubbing Eyebrow Makes Red

(Usage) If B moves right foot forward and catches the collar under A's chin, A bends left elbow and hits the inside of B's right elbow outward with left hand while left foot ahead (*Diagram 64*). At the same time, changes feet with right foot ahead while turning body. Then right palm rubs and goes forward from the end of A's own eyebrow to hit the bridge of B's nose straightly. (*Diagram 65*)

(Purpose) 1. It is quite easy to make B bleed that A's right palm rubs and goes forward from the end of A's own eyebrow to hit the bridge of B's nose, so it is called "The hitting of Rubbing Ezebrow Makes Red".

2. A hits the inside of B's right elbow outward with left hand while turning body, which makes B lose weight.

3. If B moves back and wants to escape, A can step or leap forward to pursue him by the same skill.

Diagram 64

Diagram 65

114

Form 43   The Yellow Dragon Stirs Water
Three Times — Right Style

(Usage) If B moves right foot forward and hits A's chest with right fist, A squeezes and presses towards B's left with left hand while left foot ahead (*Diagram 66*). At the same time, steps left leg to the outside of B's right foot, right hand hitting the right back of B's neck downward by smooth twining (*Diagram 67*), and right foot rising to sweep the inside of B's right foot horizontally. The attack in coordination with above and below makes B fall forward. (*Diagram 68*)

(Purpose) 1. A's left hand squeezes and presses B's right palm, which also breaks with vertical strength with horizontal strength, and rakes B's weight incline in order to create attacking position for A's moving right leg and hand forward.

2. A hits the right back of B's neck downward by smooth twining, or can split or cut B's ear violently, both of which can make B severely wounded.

Form 44   The Yellow Dragon Stirs Water
Three Times — Left Style

The usage and purpose are the same as those of the previous form, only in the opposite direction.

Diagram 66

Diagram 67

Form 45 Kick With Left Heel

The usage and purpose are the same as those of Form 35 in Series I.

Form 46 Kick With Right Heel

The usage and purpose are the same as those of Form 41 in Series I.

Form 47 Turn Flowers Out from the
Bottom of the Sea

The usage and the purpose are the same as those of the preceding Form 30.

Form 48 The Fist of Covering Hand and Arm

The usage and purpose are the same as those of Form 14 in Series I.

Form 49 Sweeping Leg

(Usage 1) A wrestles frontly with B while left foot ahead. If C steps

Diagram 68   *Diagram 69*

Diagram 70

Diagram 71

right foot and hugs A's both arms and chest with hands from A's rear (*Diagram 69*), A quickly sinks waist and turns body 45 degrees to the right, then hits C's right rib with right elbow. (*Diagram 70*)

(Purpose) A sinks waist to hold C's hands open by the force of holding

Diagram 72

Diagram 73

Diagram 74   Diagram 75

downward and turns body to the right, which makes C's soft rib under right armpit exposed.

(Usage 2) A shocks C's right instep with right foot while hitting C's right rib with right elbow (*Diagram 71*), and C certainly raises right foot to move back because of pains (*Diagram 72*). A takes the opportunity to turn body 180 degrees to the right, meanwhile, right elbow pushing C's right arm backward, left arm going through under armpit *(Diagram 73)*, and left foot sweeping C's left leg horizontally, which makes C fall backward (*Diagram 74*)

(Purpose) 1. A shocks C's right instep with right foot, which firstly makes C's right instep wounded, secondly makes C's left foot not steady so as to sweep horizontally.

2. There is hitting with A's elbow above and shocking with A's foot below, which makes C not give attention to both above and below.

3. A goes through under C's right armpit with left arm, which makes C's right shoulder not able to sink down and hit body incline. Then sweeps C's left foot by sweeping leg so that produces the effect of "overcoming a weight of 1,000 catties by four ounces".

Form 50   The Fist of Covering Hand and Arm

The usage and purpose are the same as those of Form 14 in Series I.

Form 51   Dash Leftward

(Usage 1) If B moves right foot forward and rush at A's chest with both hands, A makes a false step forward with right foot while moving left foot back, both fists moving in an arc first rightward, backward, then upward, forward and downward to pound C's hands. (*Diagram 75*)

(Purpose) 1. A moves left foot back not to close up with C, which can shun the dashing of B's both hands.

2. A's both hands change into fists to move in an arc just like swinging a hammer in order to increase inertia, which make B's hands shocked.

(Usage 2) While B is frightened at his hands being shocked, A takes the opportunity to move steps by the front foot bringing along the rear foot and dash forward with both fists, so makes C fall backward with face upward. (*Diagram 76*)

(Purpose) B is frightened at his hands being shocked and draws them back. A takes the opportunity to dash with both fists, which makes a surprise attack on B.

Form 52   Dash Rightward

The usage and purpose are the same as the previous form, only in the opposite direction.

Diagram 76   *Diagram 77*

Diagram 78   Diagram 79

Form 53   Thrust Reversely

(Usage 1) If B hits the left part of A's face with right fist while right foot ahead, A steps left foot and moves out the inside of B's right wrist upward with left fist. (*Diagram* 77)

(Purpose) A's left fist moves out the inside of B's right wrist, which can firstly break with the vertical strength of B's right fist and secondly prepare the next attack.

(Usage 2) In this time, if B changes right fist for palm and stretches left hand to hold A's left wrist with both hands, then moves right leg back and presses downward violently with hands (*Diagram* 78), A takes the opportunity to step right leg to insert obliquely under B's crotch, left fist drawing outward smoothly, right fist thrust down along the inside of B's left hip (*Diagram* 79). Then hits B's left arm and chest with shoulder leaning to make B fall outward. (*Diagram* 80)

(Purpose). 1. A steps right leg to insert obliquely under B's crotch in order to withstand the inside of B's left leg, which makes B not able to draw crotch in and not easy to stand steady so as to lighten B's pressing force.

2. A's left fist draws outward, which makes B's body incline.

3. A's shoulder leans hitting while right fist thrusting down along the inside of B's left hip. The concerted attact above and below makes B impossible to defend effectively.

Diagram 80   *Diagram 81*

Form 54   Turn Flowers Out From the
Bottom of the Sea

The usage and purpose are the same as those of the preceding Form 30.

Form 55   The Fist of Covering Hand and Arm

The usage and purpose are the same as those of Form 14 in Series I.

Form 56   Attack Twice With Forearm (1)

(Usage 1) A is wrestling with B with left foot ahead and right foot behind. If C behind A suddenly steps right foot and stretches right fist to attack towards the right part of A's back (*Diagram 81*), A immediately turns
body to the right, and bends right arm to move out C's right arm. (*Diagram 82*)

(Purpose) 1. A turns body, which can make C's right fist come to nothing.

2. A bends right arm to move out C's right arm, which makes C's body
incline and not stand steady.

(Usage 2) In this time, if C's right fist changes for palm to slip down
and press A's right wrist (*Diagram 83*), A step right foot by the stepping skill,

Diagram 82

Diagram 83

Diagram 84

Diagram 85

left fist raising C's right forearm, right fist hitting the right part of C's chest. (*Diagram 84*).

(Purpose) 1. A uses the stepping skill in order to both move quickly and build up strength.

2. A's left fist raises C's right forearm to make C's breath float up, and

122

A's right fist hits C's chest to make C's breath stop up.

(Usage 3) Follow above, if C quickly moves right foot back and presses A's right wrist down (*Diagram 85*), A immediately steps left foot and stretches left fist to raise C's left forearm (*Diagram 86*). Then, steps right foot to the rear of C's left foot and hits the left part of C's abdomen with right fist. (*Diagram 87*)

(Purpose) 1. A fist steps left foot, then right foot, which is the stride skill to pursue C.

2. A raises C's left forearm with left fist which makes C's left abdomen exposed so as to hit it with right fist.

Form 57   Attack Twice With Forearm (2)

The usage and purpose are the same as those of the previous form.

Diagram 86

Diagram 87

Form 58   Linking Cannons

(Usage) If B moves right foot forward and hits A's left temple with right fist, A immediately stretches left fist to hit the inside of B's right elbow (*Diagram 88*), and steps right foot to hit B's chest with right fist. (*Diagram 89*)

123

Diagram 88　　　　　　　　Diagram 89

(Purpose) 1. B's right fist moves an arc to hit A's left temple, which is farther than A's left fist hits the inside of B's right elbow straightly, so although B moves first, A arrives more early than B.

2. This strike has the meaning of breaking with horizontal strength with vertical strength, too.

3. A blocks B's right fist outward with left fist in order to create conditions for stepping right foot to attack B's chest with right fist.

Form 59　The Jade Girl Works at Shuttles

The usage and purpose are the same as those of Form 54 in Series I.

Form 60　The Cannon of Turning Head

(Usage) If C suddenly jump up to rush at A from the rear while A wrestling with C frontly (*Diagram 90*), A quickly steps left foot while turning body to the right and moves right foot back, at the same time, swings both palms to pound C's forearms (*Diagram 91*). Then, steps left foot again with right foot follow closely, using treading steps to hit B's chest with both fists. (*Diagram 92, 93*)

Diagram 90

Diagram 91

Diagram 92

Diagram 93

(Purpose) 1. It is swift and violent that B jumps up to rush at A from the rear. A immediately steps left foot, removes right foot and quickly turns body, which can pull open the distance.

2. A attacks B's chest with treading steps in order to build up explosive force.

Form 61   The Jade Girl Works at Shuttles

The usage and purpose are the same as those of Form 54 in Series I.

Form 62   The Cannon of Turning Head

The usage and purpose are the same as those of the preceding form 60, only in the opposite direction.

Form 63   The Fist of Putting Fists
Aside Before Body

The usage and purpose are the same as those of the preceding Form 14.

Form 64   Twist Elbow

(Explanation) According to the wrestling of *Taijiquan*, whichever arm going out of a square is called out of corners, while it going into a square is called into corners. When the other party goes out of corners, use hitting downward and horizontally; when he goes into corners, use hitting with elbow

Diagram 94   *Diagram 95*

Diagram 96   The reverse side of Diagram 96

and leaning with shoulder. The following three Forms are all the skill of hitting with elbow, just as engaging in close combat and fighting a quick battle to force a quick dicision, so as to make the other party impossible to make changes.

(Usage 1) If B moves right foot forward and stretches right fist to hit the left part of A's chest, A twines smoothly B's right wrist with left hand from inside to outside (*Diagram 94*). At the same time, steps right foot under B's crotch, left hand hugging right fist to help right arm, right elbow hitting horizontally B's waist and abdomen. (*Diagram 95*)

(Purpose) 1. A's left hand twines smoothly B's right wrist from inside to outside while B's right fist hitting the left part of A's chest in order to move out B's strength and make B's chest exposed, which creates conditions for hitting with elbow.

2. A steps right foot in order to build up the strength of hitting with elbow.

(Usage 2) If B closes chest and presses A's right forearm down with both hands at the same time, using strength towards A's left outside (*Diagram 96, the reverse side of Diagram 96*), A presses and squeezes the outside of B's right hand with left hand. Then, A's right elbow slips with a downward arc to hit B's right elbow and waist by the spiral strength and treading steps. (*Diagram 97, the reverse side of Diagram 97*)

(Purpose) A's left hand presses and squeezes the outside of B's right hand, which makes B's right rib exposed so as to slip right elbow to hit it.

127

Diagram 97	*The reverse side of Diagram 97*

Form 65   Smooth Elbows

(Usage) If B moves left foot forward and hit the left part of A's chest with left fist, A first sticks the outside of B's left wrist with left fist while left foot ahead (*Diagram 98*). At the same time, both fists cross in front of chest with right fist outside while stepping right foot to the inside of B's left knee, and right arm runs upward upon the inside of B's left arm (*Diagram 99*). Then A parts both elbows smoothly and hits the left part of B's chest with right elbow. (*Diagram 100, the reverse side of Diagram 100*)

(Purpose) 1. A sticks the outside of B's left wrist with left fist, which makes B's weight incline and fall forward so as to create conditions for right foot moving forward and right elbow going through.

2. A steps right foot to the inside of B's left knee, which makes B's left leg form separate strength and not able to close.

3. A's right arm runs upward upon the inside of B's left arm, which makes B not able to sink left shoulder and elbow down. In that case, B's breath is easy to float up.

4. In this skill of hitting with elbow, parting both elbows smoothly at the same time is for building up the outward force, but right elbow is chief, and left elbow plays a role of helping right elbow.

Diagram 98

Diagram 99

Diagram 100

The reverse side of Diagram 100

Form 66　The Elbow of Hitting Heart

(Usage 1)　If B moves right foot forward and hits A's face with right fist, A first moves out B's right fist from inside to outside with left hand while left foot ahead (*Diagram 101*).　B then hits A's face with left fist, A steps right foot

Diagram 101   *Diagram 102*

to B's crotch and bend right elbow to hit the outside of B's left forearm, meanwhile, draws B's left wrist with left hand. (*Diagram 102*)

(Purpose) 1. It is vertical strength that B's right fist hits A, and it is
horizontal strength that A's left hand moves out from inside to outside, so
horizontal strength breaks with vertical strength. Meanwhile, A makes B's
chest exposed.

2. A bends right elbow to hit the outside of B's left forearm while B
attacking A with left fist, which makes B's body incline towards the right rear
and not stand steady.

(Usage 2) In this time, A's left hand holds B's left fist and right elbow
twines adversely beneath B's left arm (if B's left arm high, beneath it; if B's
left arm low, upon it) to hit B's heart. (*Diagram 103*)

(Purpose) A holds B's left fist with left hand, which makes the part of
B's heart exposed so as to hit it with right elbow.

Form 67　The Cannon Out of Bosom

(Usage) If B moves right foot forward and hits the right part of A's
chest with right fist, A's right fist twines smoothly from below to outside
along B's right forearm forward to hit B's chin (*Diagram 104*). At the same
time, uses treading steps and stretches left fist to hit B's right soft rib. (*Diagram 105*)

130

Diagram 103

Diagram 104

Diagram 105

(Purpose) 1. A's right fist twines smoothly from below to outside along B's right forearm to hit forward, which firstly twines out B's right fist, and secondly hits B's chin. At the same time, makes B's right soft rib exposed.

2. A uses treading steps while stretching left fist to hit B's right soft rib in order to build up explosive force.

Form 68   Go Straight with left palm into Well

The usage and purpose are the same as those of the preceding Form 10.

Form 69   Plum Blossoms Scattered by the Wind

The usage and purpose are the same as those of the preceding Form 11.

Form 70   Buddha's Warrior Attendant Pounds Mortar

The usage and purpose are the same as those of Form 2 in Series I.

Form 71   Closing Form

The same as the last form in Series I.

Diagrams of
the Taijiquan Pushing
with Smooth Steps of
the Chen-Style Taijiquan

There are neither fixed patterns nor series in proper order in *Taijiquan* Pushing. Although it is full of variety, it is not out of the thirteen-character formula: to push, to pull, to squeeze, to press, to twist, to hold, to elbow, to lean, to advance, retreat, to attend, to look and to fix. To practise *Taijiquan* is to know yourself; to exercise *Taijiquan* Pushing is to know the enemy. Know yourself and know the enemy, and you can fight a hundred battles with no danger of defeat. When beginning to learn how to exercise *Taijiquan*, you have to have fixed patterns, but if you keep on exercising, "practice makes perfect", you can then proceed into the boundary of "No person knows me, only I know him" and "After understanding, the more you practise, the better you will be master. Study by memory and figure it out, little by little, and you will have your own way". The *Taijiquan* Pushing of the Chen-style *Taijiquan* is only with smooth steps and there is the great pulling with free steps in it. Now state with diagrams as follows:

Diagram 1

1. A and B stand face to face with one metre apart. (*Diagram 1*)

2. B moves left foot forward and A steps right foot to the inside of B's left foot, two knees sticking each other.

3. B stretches left hand first, and A also stretches left hand to the outside of B's left wrist to push it. Then, A's right hand places to the outside of B's left upper arm. This is for A to push.

4. A's right leg opens B's left leg by the force of knees' pushing out while A pushing B, which makes B's leg not able to draw crotch in.

5. B's right hand places to the inside of B's left upper arm to block A's right hand. (*Diagram 2*)

6. B's left arm moves a downward arc, and left hand takes the opportunity to pull the outside of A's right upper arm. At the same time, right hand holds A's right wrist and moves a rightward, downward arc. This is for B to pull.

7. B's left knee turns a small circle to kneel and press on the backside of A's knee joint while pulling. (*Diagram 3*)

8. A stretches left hand to place the inside of A's right forearm squeezing B's chest by twining, keeping the posture down, sinking waist, relaxing shoulder with elbow down. This is for A to squeeze.

134

Diagram 2

Diagram 3

9. A's knee turns a small circle to escape from B's knee's kneeling and pressing by smooth twining. Then, opens B's crotch with hip. (*Diagram 4, the reverse side of Diagram 4*)

10. While A squeezing B's chest, B's left hand places on A's right elbow joint, and right hand places on the back of A's right hand. Then, closing chest,

Diagram 4

The reverse side of Diagram 4

Diagram 5   *The reverse sido of Diagram 5*

right hand draws, moving a downward arc, to press forward towards A. This is for B to press.

11. A turns knee by smooth twining and again presses the backside of B's knee joint. The direction of B's knee is inward, but the pressing is towards A's left, so there is the outward meaning. The pressing and knee are in the opposite direction. (*Diagram 5, the reverse side of Diagram 5*)

12. While B pressing A, A relaxes waist to use the skill of smooth twining, turning wrist while moving shoulder back, and holding back B's right wrist with right hand. At the same time, moves right foot back, right hand greatly pulling B's right arm, and left hand placing to the outside of B's right upper arm to help it.

13. B then steps right leg to the inside of B's left leg, sticking and pushing it, and takes the opportunity to hold the fingers of A's left hand with left hand by the skill of adverse twining. At the same time, greatly leans to hit A's upper arm with shoulder.

14. A's right hand twists the fingers of B's right hand downward by adverse twining, and left forearm moves down to help the twisting force. This is for A to twist. (*Diagram 6*)

15. B takes the opportunity to relax waist, right arm drawing A's right hand outward, and left hand still holding A's left wrist. This is for B to hold. (*Diagram 7*)

16. In this time, A is reduced to inferiority. A holds B's right wrist to follow smoothly towards the place below B's right rib. B takes the opportunity

136

Diagram 6

Diagram 7

Diagram 8

The reverse side of Diagram 8

to open crotch with right foot outward and moves right foot back. A's right foot follows closely to the inside of B's left leg, sticking it with knee. Then, A looses right hand and hits the left part of B's chest with elbow's going through. (*Diagram 8, the reverse side of Diagram 8*)

Diagram 9   *The reverse side of Diagram 9*

17. While A's elbow hitting, B's right hand takes the opportunity to press down A's right wrist, and moves a downward arc to draw towards A's right rear and in front of the right part of A's chest. At the same time, left hand holds A's left wrist to draw towards B's right front, and moves shoulder forward to squeeze and lean A. (*Diagram 9, the reverse side of Diagram 9*)

Diagram 10

Diagram 11

18. While B squeezing and leaning the right part of A's chest, A closes
chest. At the same time, A's left hand draws B's wrist outward, and right
hand pushes and presses the outside of B's left shoulder, forming the pushing
posture. (*Diagram 10*) As above, moves in endless cycles. (*Diagram 11*)

Part II:

The Names of the Forms in the Chen-Style *Taijiquan* of Thirty-Eight Forms

Written and Performed by
Chen Xiaowang

The Names of the Forms in the Chen-Style Taijiquan of Thirty-Eight Forms

Section 1

1. Preparing Form
2. Buddha's Warrior Attendant Pounds Mortar
3. The White Crane Spreads Its Wings
4. Move Three Steps Forward
5. Walk Obliquely
6. Brush Knee
7. Wade Forward and Twist Step on Both Sides
8. The Fist of Covering Hand and Arm
9. The Punch of Draping Over Body
10. Double Push Hands

Section 2

11. Change Palms Three Times
12. The Punch at Elbow's Bottom
13. Step Back and Whirl Arms on Both Sides
14. Step Back and Press Elbow
15. Beast's Head Pose

16. Flash the Back

17. Wade Forward and Twist Step on Both Sides

18. The Blue Dragon Goes Out of Water

19. The Punch of Hitting the Ground

20. Double Raise Foot

21. The Fist of Protecting Heart

22. Forward Trick

23. Backward Trick

24. Kick With Right Heel

25. Kick With Left Heel

26. The Jade Girl Works at Shuttles

27. Lazy About Tying Coat

28. Six Sealing and Four Closing

29. Single Whip

30. The Dragon on the Ground

31. Step Forward With Seven Stars

32. Small Catching and Hitting

33. Wave Hands

34. High Pat on Horse

35. Double Wave Lotus

36. The Cannon Right Overhead

37. Buddha's Warrior Attendant Pounds Mortar

38. Closing Form

The Chen-Style Taijiquan
of
Thirty-Eight Forms

The Chen-style *Taijiquan* is originated in Chenjiagou, Wenxian County, Henan Province. Chen Xiaowang is a descendant of the nineteenth generation, who won the gold plate twice at the National Games of Wushu Discussion, Emulation and Exchange in 1980 and in 1981.

The Chen-style *Taijiquan* of thirty-eight forms was created and compiled by Chen Xiaowang at the base of the Chen-style "Lao Jia" (old frame) of seventy-four forms and "Xin Jia" (new frame) of eighty-three forms. In the process of creating and compiling, he deleted too many repeated actions and simplified too difficult ones, but still reserved the characteristics of the former attack-defence contents and twining strength. The whole series is divided into four sections and there are nine actions in each one. The distance of practising each section is 4-5 metres long with two round trips and comes back to the original place at the end of the fourth section. It will take 3-4 minutes to practise the whole series. There are two practising methods of vigour and gentleness in actions of jumping up and putting strength forth in the series, one can select according to the condition of one's own body.

SECTION 1

Form 1   Preparing Form

Stand naturally upright with feet parting a little wider than shoulder, toes pointing slightly outward, arms hanging naturally. Look forward and chest faces north. (*Diagram 1*)

Points to remember:

The Preparing Form is the preparation in consciousness and posture before the action begins. It asks: Solid spirit inside and show ease outside; Hold head naturally erect as if there is a thing on the top and not make it fall down; close lips and teeth slightly with chin drawn slightly inward; relax and sink shoulder; draw chest in and keep it naturally upright with waist down; keep back erect; open crotch and have the meaning of a round; bend both knees slightly; stand not very erect; relax the whole body; sink breath into abdomen.

The above-mentioned points must be paid attention to all the time, not only in Preparing Form but also in all actions of the whole series. Moreover,

Diagram 1

Diagram 2

as mentioned above, there are respective requirements at all respects, but they exert influence on each other. For example, as shoulder relaxed and sunk, it is easy to be done that draw chest in with waist down, solid spirit inside, sink breath into abdomen, and hold head naturally erect; as knees are bent, it is easy to be done that open crotch and have the meaning of a round.

Form 2   Buddha's Warrior Attendant
Pounds Mortar

1.   Raise arms slowly forward and upward to shoulder level with elbows bending slightly and palms facing downward. At the same time, knees bend slightly, and weight descend. Look forward. (*Diagram 2*)

2.   As weight descend, press palms slowly downward to navel level. Turn body slightly to the left and shift weight slightly to the right. At the same time, left palm twines adversely and right palm twines smoothly. (*Diagram 3*)

3.   While weight continues to shift to the right and descend, palms still push upward to the left with left twining adversely and right twining smoothly. Left palm is a bit higher than shoulder with palm facing outward and fingertips inclining upward. Right palm is a bit lower than shoulder with

Diagram 3   Diagram 4

palm upward and fingertips towards the left front. Look at the left front and chest faces northwest. (*Diagram 4*)

4. Turn body to the right. Meanwhile, shift weight to the left and turn the toes of right foot outward. Right palm changes twining smoothly for twining adversely and left palm changes twining adversely for twining smoothly. Chest faces north. (*Diagram 5*)

5. Continue to turn body to the right and shift all weight on to left leg. With body turning, palms twine to the right side of body. Raise right palm upward to shoulder level with palm facing outward and fingertips inclining upward; left palm is a bit lower than right one with palm facing upward and slightly backward, and fingertips forward. Both palms are 40 centimetres apart. Then shift all weight on to right leg and raise left foot. (*Diagram 6, 7*)

6. Slightly squating down, raise the toes of left foot and move the inside of heel forward towards the left front (about 45 degrees), heel coming down on floor. At the same time, there is the meaning of pushing upward for palms to go slightly towards the right rear. Look at the left front. (*Diagram 8*)

7. Turn body slightly to the left and shift weight on from right leg to left leg, resting the toes of left foot on floor. At the same time, while left palm changing from smooth twining to adverse twining, right palm change from adverse twining to smooth twining and stretches out towards the right rear, then with body turning, twines from back to front before abdomen. Look

Diagram 5   *Diagram 6*

147

Diagram 7

Diagram 8

towards the left front. (*Diagram 9*)

    8. With body turning to the left, shift all weight on to left leg. Move right foot a step forward, resting its toes on floor. At the same time, palms continue forward with left palm twining adversely and right one twining

Diagram 9

Diagram 10

smoothly. Faise right palm forward while right foot steps; bend left elbow and left palm squeezes forward with palm facing downward. While raising right palm forward, left palm first turns wrist to rise then close inward, placing it on right forearm and palm facing downward; both palms forming combined strength. Look forward and chest faces north. (*Diagram 10*)

9. Change right palm for fist and twines smoothly from outside to upside with fist facing inward. Left palm turns from inside to outside and sinks down with palm facing upward. At the same time, slightly squat down and raise right foot. Look forward. (*Diagram 11*)

10. After left palm falls in front of abdomen, right palm falls onto left palm. Meanwhile, right foot treads onto floor shocking beside left foot. (*Diagram 12*)

Points to remember:

1. The twining strength is the core of *Taijiquan* and it is united by two opposite basic twinings. Any action of the whole series cannot leave the twining strength all the time, so it runs through the processes of all actions. There are smooth twining and adverse twining in all actions of the whole series, so they are the basic twinings with universality; while inward and outward, upward and downward, leftward and rightward, forward and backward, greatly and slightly, all these twinings describe the different points of the twinings of all actions in direction and degree, so they are the bearings and twinings with particularity.

Diagram 11   *Diagram 12*

149

The smooth and adverse twining have not only a single pair of bearings, but according to the requirements of all actions, some are single, for example, the smooth twining of leftward and rightward; some have both the difference of upward and downward and the difference of inward and outward.

2. This form goes through the use of five pairs of twinings. The last pounding (shocking with foot and right fist hitting down left palm) is the end of this form.

3. The role of shocking with foot is to make the breath of the whole body sink down and good for blood circulation. For example, if you feel tired because of standing too long, but cannot move about under certain circumstances, you can raise heels with their toes resting on floor, and then fall to shock slightly. Thus doing some times, you can achieve the same effect of recovering from fatigue. Moreover, it can be decided according to the age and body of yourself whether shock with foot lightly or heavily, but however lightly or heavily, you must keep the strength of sinking down straight. Whether your strength is straight or not can yet be judged with the sound of shocking.

4. All actions of *Taijiquan* are asked "to hold shoulders and elbows down". "Shoulders down" has been explained in Preparing Form; "elbows down" means that in all actions, arms cannot be erect and elbows should keep winding to a certain extent with the tip of elbow having the meaning of falling down.

5. The palm in the Chen-style *Taijiquan* is asked that fingers bend backward, namely, besides thumb, other four fingers bend slightly towards the back of hand (see the shape of palm in *Diagram*). In that case, not only can concentrate breath into the tips of fingers but also can prevent arm from using stiff strength.

6. When moving left foot out towards the left front, weight must be kept on right leg. Left foot should move lightly but not float up while it moving out lightly with heel coming down on floor. There are all such requirements for every moving foot forward at first in the Chen-style *Taijiquan*.

Form 3   The White Crane Spreads Its Wings

1. Turn body slightly to the left then to the right, and shift weight to the right. At the same time, change right fist for palm to twine adversely upward to the top of head level with palm facing forward and fingertips towards the left upside; left palm twines adversely downward until it is in front of left hip with palm facing downward and the tips of fingers towards the right front. Look forward and chest faces north. (*Diagram 13*)

2. Shift all weight on to left leg, and raise right foot to move out towards the right front (about 45 degrees). At the same time, palms all twine smoothly to cross in front of chest, left palm above and right one below, both palms facing upward, fingertips of left palm towards the right front and those of right one towards the left front. Look at the right front and chest faces northwest. (*Diagram 14*)

3. Turn body to the left and the toes of right foot inward. Shift weight on from left leg to right leg. At the same time, both palms twine adversely with palms facing downward. Then move left foot back and rest its toes on floor beside right foot. Meanwhile, palms twine adversely in different direction, raising right palm until it is a bit higher than the top of head with palm facing forward and fingertips upward; while left palm moves downward un-

Diagram 13

Diagram 14

Diagram 15   *Diagram 16*

til it stops beside left hip with palm facing downward and the tips of fingers forward. Look forward and chest faces west. (*Diagram 15, 16*).

Form 4   Move Three Steps Forward

1. Turn body slightly to the left. At the same time, right palm twines smoothly forward and left one twines adversely backward. Look forward. (*Diagram 17*)

2. Then turn body to the right. Left palm twines from adversely to smoothly, and from backward to forward until it stops at the left front with palm facing the right front and fingertips upward; right palm twines from smoothly to adversely, and from forward to backward until it stops beside right hip with palm facing downward and the tips of fingers forward. At the same time, raise left leg. Look at the left front and chest faces west. (*Diagram 18*)

3. Squat slightly down and move left foot out towards the left front (about 45 degrees) with heel coming down on floor. Right palm twines adversely backward, and left palm goes slightly forward. Look forward and chest faces northwest. (*Diagram 19*)

4. Turn body to the left and shift weight on from right leg to left one with right heel coming down on floor. At the same time, left palm changes smooth twining for adverse twining from front to back with palm facing down-

152

Diagram 17

Diagram 18

ward and fingertips forward; right palm changes adverse twining for smooth twining from back to front with palm facing forward and fingertips upward. Raise right foot to move out towards the right front (about 40 degrees). Look the right side of body and chest faces southwest. (*Diagram 20*)

Diagram 19

Diagram 20

Diagram **21**　　　　　　　*Diagram* **22**

5. Turn body to the right and shift weight on to right leg with heel coming down on floor. Left palm changes smooth twining for adverse twining from backward to forward until it is at the left front; right palm changes smooth twining for adverse twining from forward to backward until it stops beside right hip. Raise left leg and chest faces west. (*the same as Diagram 18*)

Points to remember:

This Form is completed in moving steps forward continuously. While moving right leg forward, keep weight on to left leg. Pay attention to distinguishing false or true of legs and leading hands with body. While moving a step forward, body should keep original height and erect. The whole action should be round, full and natural without breaking off of the internal strength.

Form 5　Walk Obliquely

1. Squat slightly down, and move left foot out towards the left front (about 45 degrees). Turn body to the left, bending knee and shifting weight on to left leg, and right leg straightens with heel pressing down on floor to form a left "bow step". At the same time, left palm changes smooth twining

Diagram 23   Diagram 24

for adverse twining, past abdomen and left knee, and while it rises until it stops a bit higher than shoulder, bunch fingertips and turn them downward from wrist to form a "hooked hand"; right palm continues to twine adversely from outward to inward with right arm bending to pass by right ear with palm facing right ear. Look forward and chest faces west. (*Diagram 21, 22, 23*)

2.   The posture (*Diagram 24*) should be paid attention to as follows: right palm continues to twine adversely to pass by left hand from the left front to the right, separating itself from left hand.   Look at the right side of body.   Then keep right hip relaxed while turning body slightly to the left, holding shoulders and elbows down with breath sinking into abdomen. Look forward and chest faces west. (*Diagram 24*)

Points to remember:

1.   While from Diagram 21 to Diagram 22, pay attention to keeping body and head erect, and not bending waist.

2.   The posture (*Diagram 24*) should be paid attention to as follows: join inside and outside; both open out external feature and join forces the whole body.   Namely, join left and right horizontally, above and below vertically.   The former means to join hands, elbows, shoulders, hips, knees and feet; the latter means to join hands and feet, elbows and knees, shoulders and hips.

155

Diagram 25   Diagram 26

Form 6 Brush Knee

1. Change hooked hand for palm, and both palms move upward with fingertips face-to-face and palms facing forward. Look forward and chest faces northwest. (*Diagram 25*)

2.   Both palms twine smoothly to close towards in front of the left part of chest while weight sinking down. Right palm is beside left forearm with both palms facing upward and fingertips forward. Look forward. (*Diagram 26*)

3. Turn body slightly to the right and shift weight fully on to right leg. While turning body, raise left foot with the tip naturally down, and bend left knee slightly so that thigh is level. At the same time, palms twine adversely downward with palms facing downward. Look at the direction of fingertips and chest faces northwest.(*Diagram 27, 28*)

Points to remember:

1. It is asked for actions in *Taijiquan* that "down in order to up" and "up in order to down", so moving palms upward is the procedure of the drawing strength that "up in order to down".

2. *Diagram 28* is the posture of standing on one leg with combined strength, which is quite difficult. If you want to keep weight steady, the key is that keep head and neck erect; sink breath into abdomen; join forces the whole body; and pay attention to little fingers of hands while palms twining adversely.

156

Diagram 27

Diagram 28

Form 7　Wade Forward and Twist Step on Both Sides

1.　Then raise left knee slightly upward, meanwhile, palms twine down towards the right side with right palm smoothly and left one adversely. Look at the left and chest faces northwest. (*Diagram 29*)

Diagram 29

Diagram 30

Diagram 31   *Diagram* 32

2. Left foot falls down towards the left side with heel coming down on floor and toes facing the left front obliquely, and turn body to the left. At the same time, left palm twines smoothly until it is in front of chest with palm facing the right front; right palm twines smoothly until it stops on the left wrist with palm facing the left front, crossing both wrists. Look forward and chest faces west. (*Diagram 30*)

3. Continue to turn body to the left and shift weight on to left leg with left heel coming down on floor. While turning body, palms twine with left adversely and right smoothly until left palm faces outward and right one inward. Move right foot out towards the right front (about 40 degrees) while turning body slightly to the left, and shift weight on from left leg to right one with right heel coming down on floor. With body turning, both palms twine adversely until palms face downward, and then open out towards the left and right with palms facing outward and fingertips upward. Look forward and chest faces southwest. (*Diagram 31, 32, 33, 34*)

Points to remember:

1. While raising left knee (*Diagram 29*), that weight slightly sinks down, and palms twine down towards the right side should be symmetrical with left knee rising up so as to keep body in balance.

2. While palms stop to the right side of body and then in front of

Diagram 33

Diagram 34

chest, the internal strength should not be discontinued; join forces while cross both arms and then open out towards the left and right; pay attention to thumbs of both palms while opening out; at the same time, weight slightly down and breath into abdomen.

Diagram 35

Diagram 36

Diagram 37   Diagram 38

Form 8   The Fist of Covering Hand and Arm

1.   While turning body to the right, raise toes of right foot slightly and turn them outward before placing the foot flat on floor; shift weight fully on to right leg. At the same time, change right palm for fist to twine smoothly until it is beside right rib with fist facing upward; left palm twines smoothly forward until it stops at the left front. Raise left leg. Look forward and chest faces west. (*Diagram 35*)

2.   Squat slightly down and move left foot out towards the left front (about 35 degrees). Look forward and chest faces northwest. (*Diagram 36*)

3.   Turn body to the left and quickly shift weight on to the left to form a left "bow step" with right leg bending slightly and not being straight. At the same time, quickly move right fist forward towards the right (about 15 degrees) with fist facing upward; withdraw left palm beside left rib. Look forward and chest faces west. (*Diagram 37*)

Points to remember:

1.   The action (*Diagram 35*) is asked that keep head and neck erect; bend right knee slightly; sink weight down; raise left knee to form symmetry with right knee; sink breath into abdomen; join left palm and right fist.

2.   To move right fist forward (*Diagram 37*) is that give out breath from abdomen; shift weight on from right to left; thrust right leg backward and quickly turn waist to the left to get off right fist so as to make breath into it.

160

Form 9 The Punch of Draping Over Body

1. Turn body to the right and continue to shift weight to the left. With body turning, change left palm for fist to move in an upward arc until it is in front of nose with fist facing rightward; right fist twines first smoothly then adversely to move a downward arc until it stops over right knee. Look at the right and chest faces northwest. (*Diagram 38*)

2. Shift weight to the right. Left palm twines adversely to move in a downward arc until it is at the side of waist; right palm twines adversely to move in an upward arc until it stops to the level a bit higher than shoulder. Then continue to shift weight to the right and turn body slightly to the left. At the same time, right fist twines smoothly and turns outward. Look at the right.(*Diagram 39, 40*)

3. Turn body slightly to the left. While turning body to the right, right fist twines smoothly from rear to front until it stops before chest with fist facing upward, then changing smooth twining for adverse twining, bend elbow and turn forearm to move in an arc until it is beside temple with fist facing outward; left fist moves in a very small round at the left side of waist to stick to it. At the same time, further hold crotch down and turn the toes of left foot inward. Look at the direction of left foot and chest faces north. (*Diagram 41*)

Diagram 39

Diagram 40

161

Diagram 41   *Diagram 42*

Points to remember:

1. This form is asked that actions must be coherent and done at one go.

2. It is asked to practise *Taijiquan* the driving hinge is waist, not the four limbs, so actions of four limbs are stagnant and short, while actions of waist are fluent and long. This form shows the above-mentioned requirement obviously. If waist serves as axis (*Diagram 40, 41*), you can turn right arm naturally and have no trouble of attending to one thing and losing sight of another.

3. Actions in *Diagram 41* are asked; the three points (right fist, the tip of left elbow and the tip of left foot) form a line.

Form 10   Double Push Hands

1. Change fists for palms to open out towards the right front. Then turn body to the left and shift weight fully on to left leg. With body turning, palms twine with left adversely and right smoothly. At the same time, raise right leg. Look forward and chest faces southwest. (*Diagram 42, 43*)

2. Squat slightly down and move right foot out towards the right front (45 degrees). Turn body slightly to the left and shift weight to the right with right heel coming down on floor. At the same time, right palm twines adversely until it is in front of chest with palm facing downward; left palm twines

Diagram 43   Diagram 44

adversely until it stops to the level a bit higher than shoulder with palm facing
outward.   Then turn body to the right and shift weight fully on to right leg.
Left palm twines from adversely to smoothly until palm faces upward, and
then change for adverse twining from rear to front; right palm continues to
twine adversely, forming combined strength to go before chest and push out
towards the right front with fingertips of both hands a bit lower than chin.
At the same time, withdraw left foot beside right one with its toes rubbing
on floor. Look forward and chest faces west. (*Diagram 44, 45, 46*)

Points to remember:

1.   While from *Diagram 44* to *Diagram 46*, pay attention to keeping
right hip relaxed and down, and avoid raising left shoulder.

2.   While pushing hands forward (*Diagram 46*), pay attention to not
shrugging shoulders, but holding shoulders and elbows down, drawing chest
in with waist down, keeping hips relaxed and down, moving breath into
fingertips.

Diagram 45   Diagram 46

SECTION 2

Form 11   Change Palms Three Times

1. Turn body slightly to the right.   Left palm twines smoothly to stretch out with palm facing upward and fingertips forward; right palm twines smoothly to withdraw inward until it is beside left elbow with palm turned obliquely upward and fingertips forward.   Look forward and chest faces northwest. (*Diagram 47*)

2. Turn body slightly to the right.   Right palm twines adversely to push out with palm facing forward and fingertips leftward; left palm and wrist sink down with fingertips upward. Look forward and chest faces west. (*Diagram 48*)

3. Turn body slightly to the right.   Left palm twines adversely past abdomen and then upward to push out with palm forward and fingertips upward; right palm twines smoothly until it is under left elbow with palm facing upward and fingertips towards the left front.   Look forward and chest faces west. (*Diagram 49*)

Points to remember:

In this form, pay attention to leading hands with body.   Although wrists are the parts which put forth strength, they are held the keys of waist. Every time change palms, pay attention to the coordination of the whole body so as to keep breath in hands coherent.

Diagram 47   *Diagram 48*

Form 12   The Punch at Elbow's Bottom

1. Turn body slightly to the left. Left palm twines adversely downward until it is beside left hip with palm facing downward and fingertips forward; right palm twines adversely upward to forehead level with palm facing for-

Diagram 49   *Diagram 50*

Diagram 51   Diagram 52

ward and fingertips upward. Look forward and chest faces west. (*Diagram 50*)

2. Continue to turn body to the left. Left palm twines first adversely then smoothly (While it goes at the rear of body, change for smooth twining) from below to rear to move in an upward arc until it stops to the level a bit higher than head with palm facing forward and fingertips upward; right palm twines smoothly downward until it is before abdomen with palm facing the left front and fingertips obliquely downward. Look forward. (*Diagram 51*)

3. Turn body slightly to the right and squat down. While turning body, bend left elbow and sink down with left palm facing leftward and fingertips upward; change right palm for fist and place it beneath left elbow with fist facing inward. Look forward and chest faces west. (*Diagram 52*)

Points to remember:

While bending left elbow and sinking down with the fingertips of left palm upward, and changing right palm for fist and placing it beneath left elbow (*Diagram 52*), there is the meaning of sinking down for left elbow and holding up slightly for right fist so as to form combined strength.

Form 13   Step Back and Whirl Arms on Both Sides

1. Turn body slightly to the right and hold weight slightly down. At the same time, left palm twines adversely forward with palm turned obliquely

Diagram 53

Diagram 54

forward and fingertips obliquely upward; right fist changes for palm to twine adversely from under left elbow upward until it is before chest with palm turned obliquely forward and fingertips obliquely upward. Look forward and chest faces northwest. (*Diagram 53*)

2. While turning body to the left, left foot moves in an arc past right ankle towards the left rear to withdraw a step and form a right "bow step". At the same time, follow left foot, left palm twines adversely downward until it is in front of left hip with palm facing downward and fingertips forward; right palm twines adversely to stretch out with palm facing forward and fingertips obliquely upward. Look forward and chest faces southwest. (*Diagram 54*)

3. Turn body to the right, and both palms twine smoothly to turn over at the same time with palms facing upward. With body turning, shift weight fully on to left leg. Then, left palm twines adversely from the left to move in a upward arc until it is beside left cheek with palm turned obliquely forward; right palm twines smoothly until it stops in front of chest. Meanwhile, withdraw right leg and look forward. (*Diagram 55, 56*)

4. While turning body to the right, right foot moves in an arc past left ankle towards the right rear to withdraw a step and form a left "bow step". At the same time, follow right foot, right palm twines from smoothly to adversely until it is beside right hip with palm facing downward and fingertips forward; left palm twines adversely under ear to push forward. Look

167

Diagram 55   Diagram 56

forward and chest faces northwest. (*Diagram* 57)

    5.   Turn body slightly to the right and then to the left, and shift weight to the right. At the same time, right palm changes smooth twining for adverse from rear to front to twine until it is beside right cheek; left palm

Diagram 57   Diagram 58

changes adverse twining for smooth and withdraw slightly inward to form combined strength with right palm. Then, while turning body to the left, left foot moves in an arc past right ankle towards the left rear to withdraw a step and form a right "bow step". At the same time, left palm twines adversely backward until it is in front of left hip; right palm twines adversely forward to push out. Look forward and chest faces southwest. (*Diagram 58, 59*)

Points to remember:

1. This form is from open to close, and from close to open; close after open, and then open again. Such special actions are finished in continuous retreat, but the continous retreat does not mean to move back swiftly. According to the requirement that "advance and retreat must be changed", there is a posture of double open and changes of the internal strength between two actions of retreat. In that case, not retreat swiftly, but continue to use the open strength of front and back. At the same time, because there are changes, it becomes that there is advance in retreat and retreat in advance; retreat is just advance and have room for manoeuvre. This form is the only one of continuous retreat in *Taijiquan*. It is asked that slight smooth and adverse twining are added in retreat; actions should be natural and circular so as not to make the internal strength break off.

2. While moving steps back, keep weight on to the front leg; while turning body, shift weight on to the rear leg.

Diagram 59

Diagram 60

Form 14   Step Back and Press Elbow

1.   Turn body to the left and shift weight from the right to the left. Left palm twines upward towards the left rear with palm facing outward; right palm twines smoothly until it is in front of chest with palm facing upward. (*Diagram 60*)

2.   Turn body to the right and shift weight from the left to the right. At the same time, right palm twines from smoothly to adversely with elbow bending until it is in front of chest with palm facing downward and fingertips leftward; left palm twines from adversely to smoothly with palm upward. Look at the right front and chest faces west. (*Diagran 61, the front view of Diagram 61*)

3.   Turn body to the left and shift weight on to left leg. While turning body, left palm twines adversely inward until the part between thumb and index finger sticks to the chest with fingertips downward; right palm twines first smoothly then adversely to move in a small round over right leg with palm facing downward and fingertips obliquely downward. Look at the right front and chest faces west. (*Diagram 62, the front view of Diagram 62*)

Diagram 61   *The front view of Diagram 61*

170

4. Right heel rises and its toes rub on floor to move past left ankle towards the left rear to step down shocking, forming a left "bow step" with toes towards the right front. At the same time, right palm twines adversely until it is in front of chest to encircle with left arm and the part between thumb and index finger stick to left elbow with palm facing downward and fingertips obliquely downward. Then right elbow puts forth strength towards the right rear with palm sticking to chest; left palm twines adversely to put forth strength towards the left front with palm facing forward. Look forward and chest faces northwest. (*Diagram 63*)

Points to remember:

1. While right palm twines first smoothly then adversely to move in a small round (*Diagram 62*), pay attention to holding shoulders and elbows down, and it is driven by turns of lumbar spine.

2. Right foot steps down shocking at the right rear; right elbow puts forth strength towards the right rear; and left palm puts forth strength towards the left front, all these three actions should be completed at the same time.

The front view of Diagram 62   Diagram 62

Diagram 63   Diagram 64

Form 15   Beast's Head Pose

1. Turn body slightly to the right and squat slightly down. Shift weight on from left leg to right leg, and draw left foot to the side of right foot with its heel raised. At the same time, right palm twines smoothly until it is before the left part of abdomen with palm turned obliquely upward and fingertips forward; left palm twines with elbow bending until it stops in front of chest with palm facing rightward and fingertips upward. Look forward and chest faces west by north. (*Diagram 64*)

2. Squat slightly down and move left foot out towards the left front (about 30 degrees). Then, turn body slightly to the left, and shift weight from the right to the left with left heel pressing down on floor to form a left "bow step". At the same time, left palm twines adversely to press down until it stops beside left hip with palm facing downward and fingertips forward; right palm stretches forward past the right part of chest to the level a bit higher than shoulder with palm facing upward and fingertips forward. Look forward and chest faces west. (*Diagram 65*)

Points to remember:

1. While drawing left leg back (*Diagram 64*), pay attention to holding shoulders and elbows down and drawing chest in with waist down so as to sink breath into abdomen and keep weight steady.

2. Right palm stretches forward (*Diagram 65*), which is done at the same time that turn body to the left and turn lumbar spine so as to make

172

breath sent out from abdomen into fingers; and it must be symmetrical with right palm for left palm to press slightly down beside left hip. At the same time, with weight slightly down, keep left hip relaxed and kick backward with right leg.

Form 16   Flash the Back

1. Turn body and shift weight to the right with left heel serving as the axis and its toes turning inward. At the same time, left palm twines smoothly to the side of left knee with palm facing forward and fingertips downward; right palm twines adversely with arm turning until it is in front of chin with palm facing forward and fingertips leftward. Look forward and chest faces northwest. (*Diagram 66*)

2. Continue to turn body to the right and shift weight on from right leg to left leg. With left heel serving as the axis, quickly turn body towords the right rear (about 180 degrees). At the same time, while turning body, right foot sweeps in half a round towards the right rear with its toes coming down on floor and then its heel steps down shocking. While turning body, right palm continues to twine adversely upward to the level a bit higher than the top of head, and then presses downward to the side of right hip with palm facing downward and fingertips towards the right front; left palm twines smoothly with arm bending and turns upward past left ear forward

Diagram 65   *Diagram 66*

to split down with palm facing rightward and fingertips upward. Look forward and chest faces east. *(Diagram 67)*

Points to remember;

1. While turning body 180 degrees, it is asked that the whole body must be coordinate and the action is done at one go. When beginning to learn, you can first turn into the posture of *Diagram 66*, and then that of *Diagram 67*; after practising the action skilfully, do it at one go.

2. It is all at the same time *(Diagram 67)* that right foot steps down shocking; right palm presses down; and left palm twines forward to split down.

Form 17   Wade Forward and Twist Step
on Both Sides

1. While turning body to the right, shift weight on from left leg fully to right leg, and withdraw left foot to raise it. At the same time, right palm twines smoothly until it is at the rear of right hip with palm facing downward and fingertips obliquely backward; left palm twines adversely until it stops in front of right hip with palm facing downward and fingertips obliquely backward. Look forward and chest faces east. *(Diagram 68)*

The following is the same as Form 7, only in the opposite direction. In Form 7, move right foot out towards northwest; in this form, towards southeast. *(see Diagram 30-34)*

Diagram 67   *Diagram 68*

Form 18 The Blue Dragon Goes Out of Water

1. Turn body slightly to the left and shift weight to the right. Left hand changes palm for fist to twine smoothly with elbow bending and withdraw until it stops in front of chest, palm facing inward. At the same time, right palm twines smoothly to encircle with left arm, holding back erect and palm turned obliquely upward. Look at the left and chest faces north. *(Diagram 69)*

2. Turn body slightly to the right and hold crotch down. At the same time, left fist twines adversely and the side of ulna rear wrist suddenly puts forth **strength** towards the left front with fist facing backward; right palm changes **smooth** twining for adverse and withdraws to stick to chest at the same speed of left fist. Meanwhile, right elbow hits towards the right side. Look at the left front and chest faces northeast. *(Diagram 70)*

Points to remember:

1. In the Chen-style *Taijiquan,* not only hands utilize twining strength, but also legs do so.

As take steps bigger and open crotch wider, this form is the most obvious example for legs to utilize twining strength. Leg's twining is: while a hand over a leg twining smoothly, this leg usually follows it to twine smoothly outward with knee; conversely, twine adversely inward with knee. Judged by the postures of this from in *Diagrams,* legs seems not to move, only arms changes actions. In fact, legs also follow them to twine.

Diagram 69

Diagram 70

2.   This form is called "out of water", because the strength to put forth has the meaning that "retreat in order to advance".   Namely, there is upward strength at the terminal or downward half a round, so it has another name: "the shaking strength out of water".

3.   The strength to put forth of this form is a kind of hitting at short distance.   While putting forth strength, pay attention to holding weight down; sinking breath into abdomen; first storing up then giving out; leading hands with body; and the action of left arm being identical with right elbow to form symmetry.

Form 19   The Punch of Hitting the Ground

1.   Turn body and shift weight slightly to the left.   Left hand changes fist for palm to twine first adversely then smoothly to move in an upward arc to the level a bit higher than shoulder with palm facing forward and fingertips upward; right palm twines adversely until it is before left chest with palm facing the left front and fingertips upward, a bit lower than left palm. Then, while turning body to the right (about 90 degrees) and turning the toes of right foot outward, shift weight fully on to right leg and raise left leg.   At the same time, both palms twine with left smoothly and right adversely while turning body to the right.   Right palm twines to the right front, the ear level, with palm facing forward and fingertips upward; left palm twines smoothly until it is before left knee with palm facing the right front and fingertips towards the left front. Chest faces southeast. (*Diagram 71, 72*)

2.   Squat slightly down and move left foot out towards the left front (about 45 degrees).   Shift weight slightly forward and left foot comes down on floor. Left palm continues to twine smoothly upward and right palm twines adversely downward (*Diagram 73*). Then, change palms for fists and turn body slightly to the right.   Left fist twines smoothly until fist faces upward; right fist twines smoothly to the side of right ear with fist faces inward. And then, while turning body to the left, squat slightly down and bend left leg. At the same time, left fist twines adversely with elbow bending to raise up to the left with fist facing downward; right fist twines adversely to hit downward in the direction of left tiptoe with fist facing inward. Look at the lower front and chest faces north by east.(*Diagram 74, 75*)

Points to remember:

1.   The focal point of this form is to reach the requirement of "coccyx being straight and concentrating mind on the top of head" in the posture of lying prostrate.

Diagram 71

Diagram 72

Diagram 73

Diagram 74

    2. While raising left fist and right fist hitting down towards left tiptoe, pay attention to turning body and making arms suitable.

    3. Before turning body to the left (*Diagram* 74), "Changing palms for fists and first turning body to the right" has the meaning that "retreat in order to advance".

Diagram 75   Diagram 76

Form 20   Double Raise Foot

1. Turn body to the right and shift weight on to right leg with left heel serving as the axis and its toes turning inward. At the same time, left fist twines adversely downward to the side of left knee with fist facing backward; right fist with turning body twines adversely upward until it is in front of the left part of chest with fist facing downward. Look at the left front and chest faces south. (*Diagram 76*)

2. Continue to turn body to the right and shift weight on from right leg fully to left leg. While turning body, withdraw right foot half a step and rest its toes on floor. At the same time, right fist with arm turning turns outward to fall down to the right side of body with fist facing upward; left palm twines smoothly from the left to the front with elbow bending upward to the upper front of left shoulder with fist facing inward. Look forward and chest faces west.(*Diagram 77*)

3. Press right foot down on floor and raise left foot forward. At the same time, left fist changes for palm to twine adversely forward with palm facing forward and fingertips upward; right fist falls down to the rear of right hip with fist facing inward. Look forward. (*Diagram 78*)

4. Right fist changes for palm to twine adversely from rear upward with arm turning to the side of right ear with palm facing forward and fingertips upward. At the same time, press left palm slightly down. Then, while left foot does not fall on floor, right foot jumps up to kick forward with instep

178

Diagram 77

Diagram 78

Diagram 79

Diagram 80

keep level and its toes forward; and right palm from rear to front meets right instep head-on at the same time. While right palm doing so, left palm from front to rear twines adversely past left hip to move in an upward arc until it is at the left rear of body, a bit higher than head, with palm facing outward and fingertips upward; then left foot falls onto floor. Look forward and chest faces west. (*Diagram 79, 80*)

Points to remember:

The action of double raising heel is for training bounce. Both feet jump up to kick out one after another, so it has another name of "double rising". The action in the Chen-style *Taijiquan* has four methods of practice, you can select according to strong or weak yourself and your purpose. Now from easy to difficult, enumerate as follows:

1. Replace double rising with one rising. Namely, kick upward only with right foot and meet right instep head-on with right palm. There is not the procedure of both feet's leaving empty, but there is still the upward strength of double rising in practice.

2. In accordance with the statements of above-mentioned actions, use big twining rounds to help body jump up and double kick.

3. reduce the twining rounds and the whole action, namely, feet leave empty to kick up one after another.

4. After the punch of hitting the ground, while turning over body, feet leave empty to kick up one after another. This is the most difficult of methods.

Form 21　The Fist of Protecting Heart

1. Right foot falls onto floor and right leg squats slightly down. Then move left leg a step obliquely towards the left rear with left knee slightly bending to form a right "bow step". At the same time, while turning body

Diagram 81　　　　　　　　　　Diagram 82

180

to the right, left palm changes adverse twining for smooth to twine from rear to front; right palm twines adversely from below to above; both palms join forces with body turning to press slightly towards the right front with palms facing the right front and fingertips upward. Look at the left front and chest faces southwest. (*Diagram 81*)

2. Turn body slightly to the left and shift weight on from right leg to left one. Withdraw right foot and rest its toes on floor. Both palms twine at the same time with left adversely and right smoothly. Left palm twines to the left front, a bit higher than shoulder, with palm facing forward and fingertips upward; right palm twines smoothly until it is in front of chest with palm facing upward and fingertips forward. Look at the right front and chest faces west.(*Diagram 82*)

3. While turning body to the left, bend left knee and move right leg back with right knee slightly bending to form a left "bow step". At the same time, with body turning, palms change for fists to twine leftward with left adversely and right smoothly. Left fist twines to the left rear, a bit higher than shoulder, with fist facing outward; right fist twines until it is in front of nose with fist facing inward. Look at the right and chest faces west by south. (*Diagram 83*)

4. Turn body to the right and continue to shift weight to the left. At the same time, with body turning, right fist twines first smoothly then adversely from above to below to move in a rightward arc until it is over right knee with fist facing inward; left fist twines smoothly inward until it stops in front of nose with fist facing inward. (*Diagram 84*)

Diagram 83

Diagram 84

Diagram 85   Diagram 86

5. Then, turn body slightly to the left and shift weight from the left to the right. With weight shifting to the right, raise right fist to the ear level with fist facing inward; turn left fist outward and downward to the left front with fist facing upward. Look forward and chest faces southwest. (*Diagram 85*)

6. Then, again turn body slightly to the left, and continue to shift weight to the right and hold it down. At the same time, left fist twines smoothly inward until it is in front of abdomen; right fist twines smoothly with arm turning and wrist bending downward until it stops in front of chest, joining forces with left fist, both fists facing inward. Look forward and chest faces southwest. (*Diagram 86*)

Points to remember:

1. This form is asked that there are many inward and outward twinings, and they should be run through in succession. It is more difficult than the preceding actions and cannot be reached this requirement unless further practise. Because of many inward and outward twinings, waist and spine play dominative roles, and of them, spine is the first. It is one of the main forms in *Taijiquan* to train twinings inward and outward smooth and adverse.

2. While practising this form, crotch is asked to keep lower. You will feel that the breath in perineum rushes upward at coccyx when shifting weight on from one leg to another.

3. While raising right fist, and turning left fist outward and down-

ward, pay attention to keeping left shoulder relaxed and down to form the posture of expanding chest.

4. The three actions that bend left knee; fists twine leftward; and move right leg back (*Diagram 83*) should be completed at the same time. These actions can also be quickly completed in jumping up, and you can select according to strong and weak yourself.

Form 22   Forward Trick

1. Turn body to the right and shift weight fully on to right leg. Draw left foot to the side of right foot and rest its toes on floor. At the same time, while turning body, fists change for palms to twine with left smoothly and right adversely. Left palm twines until it is in front of the left part of abdomen with palm facing the right front and fingertips forward; right palm twines adversely with elbow bending to the right front, the shoulder level, with palm facing forward and fingertips leftward. Look at the left and chest faces west.(*Diagram 87*)

2. Squat slightly down and move left foot out towards the left side. Then, turn body to the left with left heel coming down on floor, and shift weight on from right leg fully to left leg, left foot pressing down on floor. And then, draw right foot to the side of left foot and rest its toes on floor. At the same time, left palm twines adversely with arm turning to turn upward

Diagram 87

Diagram 88

Diagram 89   Diagram 90

to the left with palm facing outward and fingertips rightward; right palm from above to below twines smoothly leftward until it is in front of abdomen with palm facing upward and fingertips forward. Look at the right front and chest faces southwest.(*Diagram 88, 89, 90*)

Form 23 Backward Trick

Turn body to the right, shift weight on to right leg with right heel coming down on floor and left heel raised. At the same time, while turning body, right palm twines adversely with arm turning to push upward to the right front, a bit higher than shoulder, with palm facing outward and fingertips obliquely upward; left palm twines smoothly downward until it is in front of abdomen with palm turned obliquely upward and fingertips forward. Look forward and chest faces southwest.(*Diagram 91, 92*)

Points to remenber:

The main points of forward trick and backward one are the turns of waist and back, ankle and knee. While revolving left and right or high and low, you must follow with whole body and run through in succession. In "Forward Trick", while turning body to the left, pay attention to keeping left hip relaxed and holding right shoulder down with knees combined; in "Backward Trick", while turning body to the right, pay attention to keeping right hip relaxed and holding left shoulder down with knees combined.

Diagram 91 *Diagram 92*

Form 24 Kick With Right Heel

1. Turn body to the left with left heel coming down on floor, and shift weight fully on to left leg. Then squat slightly down and move right foot out to the right with heel coming down on floor. At the same time, left palm

Diagram 93 *Diagram 94*

twines adversely upward until it is in front of forehead with palm facing forward and fingertips rightward; right palm twines smoothly downward until it stops over right knee with palm facing forward and fingertips obliquely downward. Look at the right and chest faces south. *(Diagram 93, 94)*

2. Then, shift weight from the left to the right to form a right "bow step" with left knee slightly bending. While shifting weight, turn body slightly to the left. Right palm twines adversely past abdomen upward with elbow bending until it is in front of right shoulder, a bit higher than shoulder, with palm facing forward and fingertips leftward; left palm twines smoothly downward until it stops over left knee with palm facing forward and fingertips obliquely downward. Look at the right front and chest faces south. *(Diagram 95)*

3. Shift weight on from right leg to left leg. At the same time, left palm twines adversely upward to ear level; right palm twines adversely rightward to ear level. In this time, both palms face forward and fingertips upward. Look at the right and chest faces south. *(Diagram 96)*

4. Then squat slightly down, and draw right foot to the side of left foot with its heel raised. At the same time, both palms twine smoothly downward until they cross in front of abdomen; left palm is above with palm facing rightward, right palm is below with palm facing leftward, and all fingertips towards the lower front. Look at the right and chest faces south. *(Diagram 97, the front view of Diagram 97)*

Diagram 97   `The front view of Diagram 97`

5. Then, palms change for fists to twine adversely upward until they encircle in front of chest with fists facing downward. Meanwhile, raise right foot. Look at right and chest faces south. (*Diagram 98, the front view of Diagram 98*)

6. Then, right foot quickly kicks rightward. At the same time, change fists for palms to separate hands and extend them sideways with palms facing outward and fingertips obliquely upward. Look at the right and chest faces south. (*Diagram 99, the front view of Diagram 99*)

Form 25.   Kick With Left Heel

1. Squat slightly down; right foot falls onto floor and its toes turn outward. Then turn body to the right (about 180 degrees) and shift weight fully on to right leg. Raise left foot to move out to the left with heel coming down on floor. While turning body, right palm twines adversely with arm turning past forehead to the right front, head level, with palm facing outward and fingertips obliquely upward; left palm follows left leg to twine smoothly until it is before left knee with palm facing the lower front and fingertips towards the left front. Look at the left and chest faces north. (*Diagram 100-102*)

2. Then turn body slightly to the left and shift weight on to left leg to form a left "bow step" with right knee slightly bending. At the same time,

Diagram 98	*The front view of Diagram 98*

The front view of Diagram 99	*Diagram 99*

left palm twines adversely past abdomen upward with elbow bending to the left front, a bit higher than shoulder, with palm facing forward and fingertips obliquely upward; right palm twines smoothly downward until it is over right knee with palm facing forward and fingertips obliquely downward. Look at the left and chest faces north. *(Diagram 103)*

Diagram 100

Diagram 101

Diagram 102

Diagram 103

3. Turn body slightly to the right and shift weight on to right leg. At the same time, left palm twines adversely leftward; right palm twines adversely upward to the level a bit higher than shoulder with both palms facing outward and fingertips upward. Look at the left and chest faces north. (*Diagram 104*)

Diagram 104   Diagram 105

4. Then, squat slightly down and draw left foot to the side of right foot with its heel raised. At the same time, palms twine smoothly downward until they cross in front of abdomen; left palm is above with palm facing rightward, right palm is below with palm facing leftward, and all fingertips obliquely downward. Look at the left and chest faces north. (Diagram 105)

5. Palms change for fists to twine adversely upward until they encircle in front of chest with fists facing downward. Raise left foot and look at the left. (Diagram 106)

6. Left foot quickly kicks leftward. At the same time, change fists for palms to twine adversely, then separate hands and extend them sideways with palms facing outward and fingertips obliquely upward. Look at the left and chest faces north. (Diagram 107)

Points to remember:

1. The elastic strength in this form is the both opening strength which comes from both drawing in. While hands both drawing in, elbow and arm have the both opening strength. At the same time, while knees bending and both drawing in, legs also have the both opening strength because crotch is rounded. This shows that arms and legs all have related strength to push out, and it is the key how to put forth strength lightly and crisply. It plays the symmetrical role for hands and foots to separate and extend sideways, so as to keep steady to a certain degree while body putting forth strength. This kind of method of putting forth strength is a good exercise to increase the elasticity

190

Diagram 106

Diagram 107

of joint ligament.

2. While kicking with heel, pay attention to keeping waist and hip relaxed; not bending waist; and keeping in accordance with palms' putting forth strength.

Form 26   The Jade Girl Works at Shuttles

1. After left foot falls down onto floor, turn body to the left (about 90 degrees). Squat slightly down and shift weight fully on to left leg. While turning body, raise right foot to the right rear of right foot with heel raised. At the same time, both palms twine smoothly until they cross in front of abdomen; left palm is below with palm facing rightward right palm is above with palm facing leftward, and fingertips all forward. Look forward and chest faces west. (*Diagram 108*)

Both palms twine adversely with wrists pushing up until they are in front of chest with fingertips towards downward. Left palm twines adversely past under right wrist from inside upward to cross with left wrist. Then, while holding weight down, keep both palms erect with wrists down to cross in front of chest; right palm is ahead with palm facing leftward and left palm is behind with palm facing rightward. Look forward and chest faces west.

Diagram 108

Diagram 109

Diagram 110

Diagram III

(Diagram 109, 110)

2. Raise right foot forward and palms rise slightly to join forces in front of chest. Then right foot steps down to move back, and left foot takes a big step forward. At the same time, while turning body, left palm pushes forward

Diagram 112   Diagram 113

horizontally to put forth strength with palm facing the left front and fingertips obliquely upward. Look at the right and chest faces south by west. *(Diagram III, 112, 113)*

3. Right after that take left heel as the axle and turn right with 180°, put right foot down with a distance of half a step away from left foot, and shift weight slightly rightward. At the same time, left palm after putting forth strength turns right with body to twine adversely to the side of left hip, palm facing downward with fingertips pointing right front. Right palm twines adversely to the right front to head's level, palm faces forward with fingertips pointing left upward. Look rightward and chest faces south and slightly west. *(Diagram 114)*

Points to remember:

1. While left foot takes a big step forward and falls onto floor, pay attention to quickly shifting weight on to left leg and bending knee. Then, while turning body to the right, keep hip relaxed; hold weight down; lead hands with body; and coordinate hands with body naturally so as to keep the balance of body.

2. If the sports ground is smaller, or you want to reduce sports capacity because of being old and infirm, you can turn body and take a step forward instead of leave empty and jump up.

Diagram 114   *Diagram 115*

Form 27   Lazy About Tying Coat

1. While turning body slightly to the left, shift weight on to left leg and draw right foot to the side of left foot. At the same time, both palms twine smoothly until they cross in front of chest, right palm facing upward and fingertips forward, left palm facing rightward and fingertips upward. Then move right foot out towards the right with heel coming down on floor, meanwhile, turn body slightly to the left. Look at the right and chest faces south. (*Diagram 115, the front view of Diagram 115, Diagram 116*)

2. Then, continue to turn body to the left and shift weight gradually on to right leg to form a right "bow step" with left knee slightly bending. With body turning, palms twine adversely until palms facing downward. Then, while turning body slightly to the right, left palm twines smoothly to turn over with palm facing upward; right palm slightly twines adversely with palm turned obliquely outward. Look at the right and chest faces south. (*Diagram 117, the front view of Diagram 117*)

3. Then continue to turn body and shift weight to the right with left tiptoe turned inward. While turning body, both palms change from combining to opening. Right palm greatly twines adversely to the right front, a bit higher than shoulder, with palm facing the right front and fingertips obliquely upward; left palm twines smoothly downward past abdomen until the part between thumb and index finger is akimbo. Then, while turning body

194

The front view of Diagram 115

Diagram 116

Diagram 117

The front view of Diagram 117

straight, adjust left hip and hold weight slightly down. Look forward and chest faces south. *(Diagram 118)*

Points to remember:

1. While forming the last posture, it is asked that adjust left hip and

195

Diagram 118   *Diagram 119*

the whole body so as to join forces naturally the whole body and sink breath into abdomen.

2. While bend right knee to form a right "bow step" and right palm twines adversely with arm turning to open out rightward, left knee and hip should be not erect. Note that hip cannot be erect in any actions of the whole series.

Form 28   Six Sealing and Four Closing

1. While turning body slightly to the right, right palm twines adversely to turn over outward with fingertips towards the left front; at the same time, left palm moves with wrist bending past chest until it is on right wrist with fingertips inward. Both palms join forces to squeeze out upward to the right. Look at the right front and chest faces southwest. (*Diagram 119, the front view of Diagram 119*)

2. Turn body to the left and shift weight on from right leg to left one. At the same time, right palm twines smoothly to rise with palm facing upward and strength concentrated into fingers; left palm twines smoothly with wrist bending past abdomen to move in an upward arc to push out to the left, a bit higher than shoulder, with strength concentrated into the back of hand and fingertips obliquely downward. Look at the right front. (*Diagram 120*)

The front view of Diagram 119

Diagram 120

2.   Continue to turn body to the left and shift weight on to right leg. At the same time, palms twine adversely to turn over and are separately placed under ears with palms facing each other and fingertips upward. Chest faces south. (*Diagram 121*)

Diagram 121

Diagram 122

197

4. Then both palms join forces to press down rightward until they are in front of right hip with palms facing downward and their parts between thumb and index finger face to face. At the same time, turn body to the right and draw left foot to the side of right foot with its heel raised. Look at the right and chest faces southwest. (*Diagram 122, the front view of Diagram 122*)

Points to remember:

1. Before palms join forces to press down, pay attention to inhaling while turning over palms and placing them separately under ears. While joining forces to press down, exhale deeply and slowly, and when finish exhaling, both palms just press down to the bottom in this form, to breathe is primary, and to act is secondly.

2. It should be driven by spine and waist serving as the axis for palms to change from close to open or from open to close. While turning left and right, keep the upper part of body erect, not bending forward and backward.

The front view of Diagram 122   *Diagram 123*

While palms press down, right palm is primary and left palm secondary. Back is full of breath and crotch is round and empty.

Form 29 Single Whip

1. Turn body slightly to the right, and then turn it back to the left. At the same time, right palm twines smoothly inward; left palm twines smoothly outward with both palms facing upward and all fingertips towards the right front. Then, change right palm for hooked hand and raise it up to the right, a bit higher than shoulder; meanwhile, draw left palm in front of abdomen with palm facing upward and fingertips rightward. While turning body left and right, left tiptoe also turns left and right. Look at the right front and chest faces south. (*Diagram 123*)

2. Then shift weight fully on to right leg and squat slightly down. Raise left foot to move out towards the left with heel coming down on floor. Look at the left. (*Diagram 124*)

Diagram 124   *Diagram 125*

Diagram 126   Diagram 127

3. Shift weight on from right leg to left leg and left sole is flat on floor to form a left "bow step". Then while turning body slightly to the right, right tiptoe turns inward; left palm rises slightly to place in front of chest then changes for adverse twining to move in a leftward arc to the left side, a bit higher than shoulder, with the end of palm slightly down. At the same time, right hand coordinates to move slightly rightward to from the opening strength. On forming "Single Whip", relax right hip and turn body straight. Look forward and take care of both sides; chest faces south. (*Diagram 125, 126, 127*)

Points to remember:

1. While from *Diagram 122 to Diagram 123*, the action can be done naturally and circularly only that it is driven by spine and waist serving as the axis. The action should be showed that strength is put forth from abdomen to right heel, and then makng use of reacting force of the ground, it rises through right leg and back into fingers of left hand. While relaxing right hip and turning body straight, it should be again showed that strength goes horizontally through back from the fingers of left hand to right hand.

2. Consciousness and breath are asked to be turned nimbly in *Taijiquan*. This form is a good example, while left hand twines leftward, consciousness is concentrated on left hand; after body turns straight, it is turned to be concentrated on right hand to form "hooked hand".

200

Diagram 128

Form 30   The Dragon on the Ground

1.   While turning body to the left, right hand changes for fist from the right to below past abdomen then rises to the left with fist facing upward; left palm changes for fist from the left to the right to twine adversely until it is over right forearm with fist facing downward; both fists join forces.   Look at the left front and chest faces southeast. (*Diagram 128, 129, the front view of Diagram 129*)

2.   Turn body slightly to the right and shift weight on from left leg to right leg.   At the same time, squat down and stretch left leg sideways.   Turn left fist outward and stretch it forward to the inside of shank with fist facing upward; turn right fist upward from the left to the right and then hold it down with fist facing upward.   Look forward and chest faces east. (*Diagram 130*)

Points to remember:

1.   This form is the only body skill of stretching leg sideways in the whole series.   If your ligament and physical strength are good, you can stretch left leg fully on floor, but you should adapt to it gradually and cannot stretch out all of a sudden so as not to be injured.

2.   The actions that shift weight on from left leg to right leg, squat down and stretch leg are completed in holding waist and hip replaced, turning body and stretch leg are completedin holding waist and hip replaced, turning body the breath; you cannot squat down with chest thrown out or with stiff strength.

201

Diagram 129

The front view of Diagram 129

Diagram 130

Diagram 131

Form 31   Step Forward with Seven Stars

Shift weight forward on to left leg to form a left "bow step" with right knee slightly bending.   At the same time, while moving body forward, left

Diagram 132

Diagram 133

fist rushes from below to above, a bit higher than shoulder, with fist facing upward; right fist opens out downward until it is over right knee with fist facing
upward. Then move right foot forward to the right front of left foot with its
heel raised. At the same time, right fist twines smoothly from the right to
below and then with right foot stepping from rear to front past the outside of
left wrist to rush up; both wrists cross in front of chest with fists facing inward. Look forward and chest faces east. (Diagram 131, 132)

Points to remember:

1. This form has another name of "The Fist of Seven Stars". What is
called "Seven Stars" means that the six parts, right fist, right elbow, right
shoulder, head, left shoulder, left elbow, and they help left fist rush up, so
seven parts in all. And while fist rushes, step forward. So it is called "Step
Forward with Seven Stars".

2. While left fist rushes up to form a left "bow step", note that right
leg puts forth strength downward and hold left hip relaxed. Body should rise
in spiral and not be pulled up.

Form 32   Small Catching and Hitting

1. Turn body slightly to the right and shift weight fully on to right leg.
While change fists for palms and right sole is flat on floor, raise left foot to
move out towards the left front (about 20 degrees) with heel coming down on

Diagram 134   Diagram 135

floor. With body turning, both palms twines adversely to separate each other. Right palm twines with arm bending to the right front, head level, with palm facing outward and fingertips obliquely upward; left palm twines until it is over left knee with palm facing downward and fingertips towards the right front. Look at the left front and chest faces southeast. (*Diagram 133, 134*)

2. While turning body slightly to the right and shifting weight slightly to the left, left sole is flat on floor. Then turn body to the right and shift weight on to right leg. At the same time, right palm twines smoothly until it is in front of the right part of chest with palm facing leftward and fingertips obliquely upward; left palm twines smoothly upward, and hold up forearm with palm facing forward and fingertips upward. Look at the left front and ches faces south. (*Diagram 135, 136, the front view of Diagram 136*)

2. While turning body and shifting weight to the left, bend left knee and right leg steps down. At the same time, right plam pushes out (puts forth strength) past chest to be placed under left elbow with palm facing leftward and fingertips upward; left palm twines adversely outward with palm facing the left front and fingertips upward. Look at the left and chest faces east. (*Diagram 137*)

Points to remember:

1. Before move out left leg, pay attention to bending knee, relaxing hip and holding weight down. The coordination of two actions that palms twine adversely to separate each other and move out left leg should be identical.

2. The last action in this form should be completed in a continuous pro-

Diagram 136

The front view of Diagram 136

Diagram 137

Diagram 138

cedure. While shifting weight to the left, bend left knee and right leg steps down. It is a short strength to be put forth that right palm pushes out past chest. Only by relaxing waist and left hip, rounding crotch, and adjusting the whole body well, can you put forth strength suddenly in the continuous procedure.

Form 33   Wave Hands

1.   Turn body to the right and shift weight on to right leg. With left heel serving as the axis, left tiptoe turns inward to form a right "bow step". While turning body to the right, right palm twines adversely upward with arm bending until it is in front of the right part of chest with palm facing downward and fingertips leftward; left palm twines smoothly downward until it stops over left knee with palm facing forward and fingertips leftward. Look at the left front and chest faces south. *(Diagram 138)*

2.   Then while turning body to the right and shifting weight on to left leg, right foot moves a step lightly to the rear of left foot. At the same time, left palm twines smoothly until it is in front of abdomen, then changes for adverse twining with arm turning past chest to move in a leftward and upward arc to the left front, a bit higher than shoulder, with palm facing the left front and fingertips obliquely upward; right palm twines smoothly downward until it stops in front of abdomen with palm turned upward and fingertips towards the lower front. *(Diagram 139, the front view of Diagram 139)*

3.   Then, turn body slightly to the right and shift weight on from left leg to right leg; right sole is flat on floor, and left foot moves a step towards the left. At the same time, right palm twines adversely past abdomen with arm turning upward and bends elbow to place itself in front of the right part of chest with palm facing forward and fingertips obliquely upward; left palm

Diagram 139

The front view of Diagram 139

Diagram 140   Diagram 141

twines smoothly downward until it is over left knee with palm facing forward and fingertips obliquely downward.   Look at the left front and chest faces south. *(Diagram 140)*.   Thus go round and begin again, moving three steps continuously.

Points to remember:

The requirement that round crotch should be paid attention to specially in the action of moving steps lightly in this form.   Only by doing the action under the circumstances of rounding crotch correctly, can you form the hidden twining strength in legs.   Otherwise, not only have no hidden twining strength, but also feel actions uncomfortable.

Form 34   High Pat on Horse

1.   Turn body to the left and shift weight fully on to left leg.   With body turning, right foot takes half a step forward towards the right front. At the same time, left palm twines smoothly until it is in front of chest with palm facing rightward and fingertips obliquely upward; right palm twines smoothly past abdomen towards the left with palm facing leftward and fingertips obliquely upward; both palms cross in front of chest with right palm below.   Then, shift weight to the right, and palms twine adversely until palms faces downward.   Look forward and chest faces southeast. *(Diagram 141, 142)*

Diagram 142   Diagram 143

2. Then turn body to the right and shift weight on to left leg. With body turning, both palms twines adversely to separate each other sideways to the level a bit higher than shoulders with palms facing the lower front and fingertips obliquely upward. (Diagram 143)

Diagram 144   The front view of Diagram 144

3. Then turn over palms to separate and extend them sideways. Turn body to the left and shift weight on to right leg with right tiptoe turned upward. At the same time right palm moves with arm turning and elbow bending until it is beneath the right part of chin with palm facing the left front and fingertips upward; left palm coordinated with right palm twines smoothly slightly inward with palm facing upward and fingertips obliquely towards the right front. Look forward and chest faces east. (*Diagram 144, the front view of Diagram 144*)

4. Continue to turn body to the left and shift weight fully on to right leg. Left foot with its tiptoe rubbing floor draws to the side of right foot and rests its toes on floor. While turning body, left palm continues to twine smoothly past under right elbow with little finger sticking body to draw towards the left inside until it is in front of the left part of abdomen with palm facing upward; right palm twines adversely to push out towards the right side to the level a bit higher than shoulder with palm facing the right front and fingertips obliquely upward. Look at the right front and chest faces north. (*Diagram 145, 146*)

Points to remember:

1. The three actions should be completed at the same time that right palm pushes out; left palm twines smoothly to draw inward; and left foot moves back. All these actions should be coordinative and identical.

2. While right palm moves with arm turning and elbow bending until

Diagram 145   *Diagram 146*

it is beneath the right part of chin, breath must be full of back and first draw the turning strength. Only by first turning enough then opening, can you put forth a pressing strength in spiral.

3. While right hand pushes forward, there should be the posture of propping up in all directions. This form is also asked that the internal strength should be continuous in twinings.

Form 35   Double Wave Lotus

1. Squat slightly down. Right palm moves up towards the left to the level a bit higher than shoulder with palm facing forward and fingertips obliquely upward; left palm moves inward with wrist bending to coordinate with right palm in front of abdomen, palm facing upward and fingertips upward. Then, while turning body slightly to the right and shifting weight to the left, left palm twines adversely from below to above; right palm twines smoothly downward with right heel raised. And then, turn body slightly to the left and shift weight to the right. Both wrists cross in front of chest; left palm is above with palm turned obliquely downward and fingertips obliquely

Diagram 147   Diagram 148

upward; right palm is below with palm obliquely upward and fingertips towards the left front. At the same time, right heel comes down on floor and left heel rises. Look at the left front and chest faces north. (*Diagram 147, 148, 149*)

Diagram 149

Diagram 150

2. Turn body slightly to the right and shift weight fully on to right leg. Squat slightly down and move left leg out towards the left front (about 45 degrees). At the same time, palms twine adversely; left palm twines downward past abdomen until it is over left knee with palm facing downward and

Diagram 151

Diagram 152

fingertips towards the right front; right palm twines upward and rightward to head level with palm facing rightward and fingertips obliquely upward. Look forward. *(Diagram 150, 151)*

3. Continue to turn body to the right and shift weight on from right leg to left leg. While turning body, palms twine with left smoothly and right adversely from the left to the right to move in an arc to the right side of body; left palm is in front of right hip and right palm is at the rear of right hip with both palms facing downward and fingertips all towards the right rear. Look at the lower right side and chest faces east. *(Diagram 152, 153)*

4. Then keep weight fully on to left leg and raise right foot towards the left front with palms swaying backward. Then right foot makes a fan-shaped swinging towards the right rear and palms meet right instep head-on from rear to front. *(Diagram 154, 155, 156)*

Points to remember:

1. While the upper part of body leans forward and foot sways, pay attention to holding waist and hip down, keeping body in balance and driving the swaying of right foot with waist serving as the axis. It can be changed for slow action to old and infirm persons, and hands need not meet instep head-on.

2. While foot sways, palms don't slap against instep, but hands and foot should meet each other head-on.

Diagram 153

Diagram 154

Diagram 155

Diagram 156

Form 36   The Cannon Right Overhead

1. After swaying outward, right foot falls down to the right rear. At the same time, palms change for fists from rear to front with arm turning to

Diagram 157

Diagram 158

twine smoothly and slightly rush forward with fists facing each other, left fist ahead, right fist behind, and both fists at the left front. Look at the right front and chest faces north by east. *(Diagram 157, 158)*

2. Then while shifting weight backward, bend both knees, squat slightly down and turn body to the right. At the same time, fists twine smoothly with wrists turning from front to below to move in an inward arc until they are in front of abdomen with left palm facing downward and right palm turned obliquely downward. Look at the left front. *(Diagram 159, 160)*

3. Turn body slightly to the left and shift weight forward to form a left "bow step". At the same time, with arms turning, fists put forth strength towards the left front with elbows slightly bending, left fist a little ahead, and both fists facing inward. Look at the left front. *(Diagram 161)*

Points to remember:

1. While fists twine smoothly with wrists turning from front to below to move in an inward arc, pay attention to relaxing shoulders and holding elbows down. While fists rush forward, keep left hip relaxed so as to turn waist and back and make strength reach fists smoothly.

2. The shaking strength is used in the action that fists stretch out towards the left front. It is the strength of short distance and must be showed as if sparks fall onto skin, thus putting forth with shaking. Old and infirm persons can change it for gentle one to practise.

Diagram 159

Diagram 160

Diagram 161

Diagram 162

Form 37 Buddha's Warrior Attendant Pounds Mortar

1. While turning body to the right, shift weight backward and bend right knee to squat down. At the same time, fists change for palms to twine with left smoothly and right adversely towards the right rear to push up to the right side of body with palms facing the right front and fingertips obliquely upward. Fingers extend but are not soft. Look forward. *(Diagram 162)*

(The following actions are the same as Diagram 9-12)

Form 38 Closing Form

1. Right fist changes for palm and both palms twine smoothly at the same time to separate sideways with palms and fingertips facing each other. Meanwhile, body slightly rises, and draw a deep breath slowly. *(Diagram 163)*

2. Palms twine from smoothly to adversely with elbows bending to sides of chest separately with palms facing downward and fingertips forward. At the same time, change inhaling for exhaling. *(Diagram 164)*

3. Then bend knee and hold hip relaxed with weight down. Palms come down until they are in front of hips with palms facing inward and fin-

Diagram 163   Diagram 164

gertips downward. At the same time, exhale slowly and deeply. Keep the whole body relaxed and into the state of rest. Chest faces north. (*Diagram 165*)

Points to remember:

1. In this form, just as in "Six Sealing and Four Closing", to breathe is

primary and to act is secondly. Actions should assist breath, and not influence it. While exhaling, note specially that first bend knees and hips to squat down, then hold body down along with them. Only thus can you breathe thinly, evenly, deeply and long; and can actions not influence breath.

2. This form is the last one of thirty-eight forms. It is finished by drawing a deep breath and then exhaling slowly, thus, making the whole body adjusted and recovered in the posture of rest. After you finish practising, you will feel happy and relaxed.

Diagram 165

Profiles of Chen Fake, Feng Zhiqiang and Chen Xiaowang

by Feng Dabiao

I. Chen Fake

Chen Fake (1887—1957), an accomplished *Taijiquan* master, was born in Chenjiagou Village, Wenxian County, Henan Province. He was the 17th generation successor of Chen family *Taijiquan*. His great grandfather was the celebrated Chen Changxing.

Fake was a fervent successor of *Taijiquan* as a heirloom. He made it a rule for himself to practise a set of 10 reps of *Taijiquan* in the morning, at noon and in the evening every day. He particularly made a point to practise in the sun in summer so that he could tell by his own shadow whether he had struck the right posture. More often than not, did he make at least 100 reps a day. Besides, he practised with a wooden staff about four metres long and 15 centimetres thick. He shook the heavy thing 300 times a day as a way to exercise his wrist strength.

Chen began to make a fame in his village when he was 17 years old. There was a very strong man nicknamed "the Bull" in his village. One day, Bull gripped Fake's wrists tightly. Chen merely resorted to the "shake" force of *Taijiquan*, with which he not only freed himself from the grip but threw

Bull to the ground. When the guy got up ad tried to reach out at him, Chen followed his opponent's movement with the *Taijiquan* movement of "the black dragon emerging from the water", sending his opponent more than three metres away on his back. The year when Chen reached 20, there was a dual fight competition of wushu, or Chinese boxing, in the county town. Chen took part and found no equals there. His fame took wings throughout the county.

When Chen Fake's name reached the warlord Han Fuju, the despot sent a man to invite Chen to his headquarters and offered to give him the post as the chief coach in Chinese boxing. Chen flatly refused the offer. This enraged the warlord who made a man thrust a spear at Chen's throat. Chen, bare-handed, waited till the spearhead was close to his throat. Then he swiftly lowered his body and, with the "swivel" force of *Taiji*, described a circle in the air with his hands, gripped the stem of the spear, twisted slightly and jabbed at the opponent with the other end of the spear stem. That man was sent three to four metres away. Still not reconciled, the warlord made Chen stand in a circle marked on the floor and told him to put his hands behind. Then he asked Chen Fake whether he could cope with a wushu coach who would try to slash at him with a broadsword. Chen said he could try. When the coach attacked Chen with a flourish of his broadsword, Chen Fake, how-ever, remained in the circle and without using his hands, just employed "the double kicks" and "double wavers" of the Chen family Tai Ji Quan routines and kicked the broadsword off from his opponent's hand.

In 1928, Chen Fake went to Beijing to teach *Taijiquan* at the invitation of his nephew Chen Zhaopi. At that time there were the three Li brothers who enjoyed some fame as Chinese boxing coaches in Beijing. The Li brothers were arrogant and never thought much about the Chen family *Taijiquan*. They learned about Chen's arrival and invited him to have a contest.

Chen arrived to find all the three Li's at home. The eldest brother, tall and squarely built, was not only haughty, but insulting in manner and conver-sation. He was the first to attack Chen. With a cry "Ha!", Chen made a lightning movement and flung the eldest Li on the windowsill beside the door. The other two Li brothers saw this and neither of them ever dared to make a move.

After this incident, Chen Fake won his fame in the ancient capital. He became hardly able to handle such a large number of callers who came to ask him to teach.

Among his callers were Xu Yushen, chief of the then Beiping Wushu Centre, and noted masters such as Li Jianhua and Shen Jiazhen. They were drawn by Chen's fame. They came, asked for a contest and through the friendly contest they came to admire Chen's excellence. With admiration, he asked Chen to teach them. The famous Peking opera actor Yang Xiaolou who was known for his mastery of Kung Fu in playing the role of heroes on the stage, also asked Chen to be his Kung Fu master. Chen's pupils were unanimous about their master's "purity" of skill. They collectively presented him a silver cup with the inscription "The Greatest In *Taiji*." After that, Chen Fake established his wushu training centre in Beijing. Gradually, the Chen family *Taijiquan* spread.

Once Xu Yusheng sponsored a wushu contest in Beijing and Chen was invited to be an adviser. At a discussion on the contest rules, someone proposed that one dueal should be limited to 15 minutes. Chen Fake suggested that three counts of "one, two, three" would be enough to decide the winner. Li Jianhua was present and he was dubious. Chen smiled. "If you don't believe, let's have a try," he said. Li stood two metres high and weighed 100 kilogrammes. Earlier he had been the wushu coach of the Northeast China University. He was rather polished with the *"bagua"* style of wushu. He approached with a movement. Chen pivoted his body a little and with a quick parry, Li was lifted some 30 centimetres from the ground and collided against the wall. A glass pane with photographs on the wall was dashed to pieces. Li was not hurt but his jacket was smeared with motar powder from the wall which had gone deep into the threads of the cloth.

At that Beijing wushu contest, Shen San, the nationally known wrestler, was also present. After exchanging some polite remarks, Shen asked Chen: "What will a *Taijiquan* master do when he is confronted by a wrestler?" Chen replied smilingly: "How could you choose your enemy?" So the two agreed to have a try as an encounter between a wrestler and a *Taiji* master. Chen raised his two arms and asked Shen to grasp them. When Shen took Chen's arms and the onlookers were expecting to see a thrilling duel, it was no more than three seconds and the two laughed. The contest was over! On the evening two days later, Chen was teaching his pupils at his training centre. Shen called, bringing Chen an expensive present. Seeing Chen's pupils were perplexed, Shen San explained, saying: "Master Chen is not only good at wushu, he is even better in morals. That evening master Chen let me hold his arms. I intended to make use of Master Chen's momentum but I couldn't. When I tried to lift my feet, I again found I could not do so. I was immediately aware of the fact that Master Chen was much better than I. Yet, Master Chen neither put me off my feet nor told anyone else. That's great. Today I am coming especially to express my gratitude." This is just one of the many instances showing Chen Fake's lofty character. He stayed in Beijing for dozens of years without creating a single enemy among the wushu circles.

Among Chen Fake's numerous pupils, many had already mastered some other forms of Chinese wushu. They included such noted wushu devouts as Liu Ruizhan, Tang Hao, Gu Liuxin, Lei Mumin, Tian Xiuchen, Li Jinwu, Feng Zhiqiang and Li Zhongyin who had already had a good mastery of some of forms of wushu before becoming Chen Fake's pupils. This is a clear indication of Chen's prestige as a master of the Chen family *Taijiquan* among the "experts".

After the founding of New China, Chen Fake cooperated with another noted wushu master Hu Yaozhen in forming the Capital Wushu Society with Chen as the president. In that capacity, he made an admirable contribution to the spreading of the Chen family *Taijiquan*. He died of illness in Beijing of the age of 70.

2.   Feng Zhiqiang

Feng Zhiqiang, born in 1926, is a native of Shulu County, Hebei Province. He is a man of strong build with thick eyebrows and big bright eyes.   In his youth, he learned *Tongbiquan* from Han Xiaofeng, a wushu master of Cangzhou, Hebei Province, and Liu He *Xinyiquan* from Hu Yaozhen, amaster of Shanxi Province.   In 1951, he began learning the Chen family *Taijiquan* from Master Chen Fake of the Chenjiagou Village of Henan Province.   While learning the No. 1 and No. 2 routines of the Chen family *Taiji*, he made special efforts to learn the "arm-push" (an exercise between two persons by pushing each other's right forearm as a basic training of strength in the arms and stance and of coordination of movement) of the Chen family *Taiji*.   At that time, none of the trainees under Master Chen dared to practise it with the master, except for Feng. This is because Master Chen's push was so powerful that before his opponent had exerted strength, the master had already shoved him several metres away. Feng, however, was not afraid of being thrown to the ground. After many falls, he finally got the knack of it. Feng fortified his every session under the coachship of Master Chen by going to the park the next morning to practise the standing exercise of the horse-riding position for two hours and 15 reps of the routines of the Chen family *Taiji*. Thus, Feng has excelled all his mates in the grappling, toppling, swinging and shaking free movements peculiar to the Chen family *Taiji*.

3. Chen Xiaowang

Chen Xiaowang was born in 1946 in the Chengjiagou Village in Wenxian County, Henan Province. He is a son of Chen Zhaoxu, the eldest son of the Chen family *Taiji* master Chen Fake. So Xiaowang is the 19th generation successor of the Chen family *Taiji*.

Chen Xiaowang was taught his family art of *Taiji* by his father Zhaoxu and his uncle Zhaokui and especially his uncle Zhaopi. As early as in his childhood, Xiaowang learned about the legendary feats of his grandfathers and saw for himself the superb kung fu of his father and uncles. All this filled the young mind with a determination to carry on the family tradition of martial art. When he was old enough to do physical exercises but still below the school age, he learned wushu almost all day long every day. When he was attending school, he persisted in practising five reps of the *Taiji* routines every morning and evening. During the busy farming seasons such as harvesting and spring sowing, when others would seize every spare minute to take a rest, Chen Xiaowang snatched every odd moments of a work break to practise his wushu. He made it a rule for himself to do at least 20 reps of the *Taiji* routines every day, shine or rain, busy or not. Once his family was building a house, Xiaowang was kept busying running around purchasing the building material. When he was back home, he even suspended the construction so that he could have time to practise his *Taiji* routines to make up for the loss of time. Thanks to his perseverance, Chen Xiaowang made rapid progress and soon stood out among the young generation of the Chen family.

In 1980, the Physical Culture and Sports Committee of Henan Province set up a wushu studio and Chen Xiaowang was made a professional coach. Since then, Xiaowang has been practising with redoubled efforts. He has thus made marked progress. For his superb skill, he won gold medals at the national wushu tournaments held in Taiyuan, Shanxi Province, in 1980 and in Shenyag, Liaoing, Province, in 1981. He appeared as a leading figure in the TV feature on his native village Chenjiagou entitled "A Trip to the Home of *Taijiquan*" made by the Henan provincial TV station.

The Chen family *Taiji* consists of two routines (the second routine is also called Pao Chui). Chen Xiaowang has been concentrating on developing a simplified version of the Chen family *Taiji* in recent years. His first product has been a simplified 38-movement *Taiji* routine which is being popularized in Henan, Shanghai and other parts of the country. This has been hailed as a blessing to all beginners of the Chen family *Taiji*.

Editor's Postscript

1. The Chen school of *Taijiquan* is one of the major branches of *wushu* in China, and it is the origin of all the other forms of *Taijiquan*. It is executed in a continuous and relaxed manner, with circular and extended movements. It requires that the mind be in command of the *qi* (the circulation of vital energy) which in turn activates the body, so as to gain the best effects and exercise both the internal and external parts of the body. This school of *Taijiquan* can be used as a means of attack or defence, and the exercises help keep the body fit and is suitable for people in all the trades and professions.

2. The book is divided into two parts. The first part contains illustrations for the first and second routines of attacking movements; the second part is the simplified *Taijiquan* of the Chen school in 38 movements for beginners.

   This book does not include the first and second routines of the Chen-style pugilistics as they have already been published in China and abroad.

3. The writer, compiler, performers and translator are all disciples of the Chen school. Feng Zhiquang is a renowned *Taijiquan* master of today and a brilliant disciple of Chen Fake, a descendant of the 17th generation of the founder of the Chen school; Chen Xiaowang, the representative of the 19th generation, is the grandson of Chen Fake; Feng Dabiao and Zhang Chundong are disciples of Chen Zhaokui, the 18th generation descendants of the Chen family and the son of Chen Fake and uncle of Chen Xiaowang. The translator Wan Wende is also a disciple of the Chen school.

   The writer of the foreword, *The Origin, Evolution and Development of Taijiquan,* is Gu Liuxin, a renowned *Taijiquan* master and a disciple of Chen Fake.